Out of the Pigpen!

Jo Wright

Onwards and Upwards Publishers

Berkeley House, 11 Nightingale Crescent, Leatherhead,
Surrey, KT24 6PD.
www.onwardsandupwards.org

Original title: An Englishwoman Abroad

ISBN: 978-1-907509-70-4
Typeface: Sabon LT
Graphic design: Leah-Maarit

Endorsements

I would thoroughly recommend reading this book. Jo writes as she experiences life, and her Christian faith is apparent throughout. Her insight into life and God at work in every sphere shows through every page.

Roger Bird
Pastor of Abbey Chapel, Tavistock
School Pastor Coordinator, Tavistock
March 2013

This book is compulsive reading, beautifully written in easy-to-read chapters. It tells of a changed life: Jo's journey through painful and difficult circumstances that bring her to the end of herself, where she finds the overwhelming love of The Father, which lifts her out of the mire and brings complete transformation and healing and purpose to her life.

Diana Wood
Lydia Prayer Ministries
February 2013

Acknowledgements

Thank you to my dear friend Sue for your help and patience in reading and helping to prepare the original manuscript. What an encouragement you are to the body of Christ.

Jo Wright
February, 2013

About the Author

Jo Wright is a primary school teacher. She lives in Tavistock, Devon (having moved from the Midlands when her oldest boy was only two). She is married to Sam and has two children from her first marriage, Kirsty and Josh, as well as being a mother to Jude who is now five years old.

She is a member of Kings Community Church in her home town and has many spiritual children, whom she helps to mature in cooperation with the expanding number in fellowship there. Her house is always open for anyone to drop in for a hot drink and a chat. She loves to have people over, and many have stayed for weekends when a babysitter was needed on street pastor duty days or just because they needed a peaceful place to sleep.

This book is dedicated to my beautiful husband, Sam, whose light shone so brightly in a dark place.

Thank you for your love, patience and kindness, and for leading me home. You're the best husband and the best father. Our family is truly blessed with you looking after us.

To Vince and Shelley and all the spiritual fathers and mothers everywhere:

Life is so much better with you in it. Thank you for your love, guidance, truth and prayers; you'll never really know how much that means to those you care for. Keep on keeping on!

Contents

"So he got up and went to his father. But while he was still a long way off, his father saw him and was filled with compassion for him; he ran to his son, threw his arms around him and kissed him."

Luke 15:20

Introduction

We are only here for a short time, but we are here on the earth at an amazing time in history. Some of us may even see Jesus' return in our lifetime.

This book was born out of a heart to see more radical disciples raised up in the body of Christ in these last days.

It's about how to live victorious, power-filled, happy Christian lives for Jesus. It's about shining our lights here on the earth as He intended us to. It's about keeping our eyes on eternity (and the heavenlies) whilst living down here for his glory.

Sometimes we feel like visitors/foreigners abroad on the earth, and I guess that's how it should be because it means we'll feel perfectly at home when we get to Heaven.

This is a book for all Christians and non-Christians who want to live a great, peaceful life. Living for Jesus fills that something that is missing in your life. Connecting with the one who created you makes you whole and makes the connections in your body, soul and spirit necessary for the most amazing journey through this life imaginable. Taste and see that the Lord is good, and I promise you will never look back.

Enjoy your amazing life, head up; you can be born again into an incredible future in the Kingdom – a kingdom where the rules of engagement depend on obeying the king of kings, to see His kingdom come on this earth.

Out of the Pigpen!

PART I

The Journey

*Important steps forward in your
relationship with Jesus*

Out of the Pigpen!

CHAPTER ONE

God is our Father

A word that was given to us as a church at the start of 2010. It applies to all churches and Christians as we move forward into the new assignments that God has for us to do in these end times.

Our Father's heart for us

A LETTER FROM HEAVEN

"I am longing to have a one-to-one chat with everyone, young or old. I am your Father who loves, cares for and disciplines his children. I know you and what you are, have been and will be. I want to talk to you and guide you.

"Listen to me. Choose to submit to me. See that listening is active, as in 1 Samuel 3:10:

> *And the Lord came and stood and called as at other times,*
> *Samuel! Samuel! Then Samuel said, Speak, Lord,*
> *For Your servant is listening.*

"I know that some of you are thinking, 'What's new?' and have always known I want to talk to you – but things have been in your way, preventing you from stepping into your inheritance. I will reveal them to you.

"Fear has stopped some of you from listening to my words, sent along within the teaching of visitors to the church and by your brothers and sisters, and you have used excuses such as lack of experience or knowledge. The personality of the person delivering the word must not stop you hearing it.

"Some of you believe that situations that you have prayed for in the past didn't turn out as you thought you were told they would, so you have guarded your hearts to prevent yourselves getting hurt. This is unbelief. You must not let the scars of the past colour your future. Come to me fresh every time. If I say something will happen and you don't really believe it in your heart, it's unbelief. The enemy loves this situation and claims many victories.

"Sometimes you put limits on me by not believing each other when anything is possible with me. There will come a time when a person saved one day will be using a given gift in churches straight away. Your friends will even come to you, having heard of me from elsewhere, and ask why you didn't tell them about me. Align yourself with my plan; *it's all in hand.* Blessings will follow.

"People-pleasing has been prevalent in my church for some time. This can take the form of routines in services, watering down your beliefs to please your parents or children. My children can only come to *know* me (not just know *about* me or have *knowledge* of me) by following all of my word because righteousness will be contested within families and outside. Jesus foretold this in Matthew 10:36:

A man's enemies will be the members of his own household.

Now is the time to listen. Now is the time to prepare yourselves for the next battle. There will always be one. Get rid of unbelief, gossip, whinging about each other and me. Trust me; always come to me first. Shift your thinking so that you see yourselves as saints not sinners.

A word from me is precious. Be encouraged, pleased, honoured to receive it and be thankful that I care so much for you that I will tell you the truth.

Begin to see a word as a love letter sent from me, your Father, delivered by your loving brother or sister.

If you need support, ask someone to come with you. Encourage each other, live your wonderful lives as my sons and daughters; then others *will* see it and want it too.

CHAPTER TWO

The Starting Line

When were you born (again)?

The starting line

When does life begin? If we think of life as a running track and the beginning of the race as a starting line then what happens before and after the line is very interesting. Before the line is the world – and in my case that was a life of working two jobs to pay a mortgage as a single parent and partying at weekends (which involved some pretty heavy use of tobacco and alcohol). I thought this was life.

This was just how it was until one day, after a particularly dodgy encounter whilst out partying, I found myself saying, "I've had enough; I'm not interested until I meet Mr Right." The rest is history. (I met and married my husband, Sam Wright!)

You see, God is waiting. He is the father in the story of the prodigal son. He is waiting for us to utter those words, "I've had enough, and I'm ready to come out of the pigpen." We must have an open heart when we do this or there will be no evidence in our lives that God has come in and changed us. (We are encouraged in the Bible to "look for the fruit".) This, I believe, is the starting line, and it is then that the journey begins for us, as we get filled with the Holy Spirit at that moment of turning. We become a new person; we become *born again*, and hopefully we will get amongst a good body of people in a church that nurtures us. It's very important, I believe, that new Christians are aware of the existence of an enemy and of his intentions to destroy.

Gradually God will reveal His purposes for us and what He would like us to do to serve in His Kingdom. By staying aligned to God's plan for the earth (which I believe is to bring in as many of the lost as we can in the last days) we can learn all sorts of things about ourselves and who we are in God. This makes us more confident to do the work for which we have been called.

A perfect example of this was how after a short period of reticence in bringing God's word, where I had succumbed to the deception that what I had to say would upset people, God told me I was a catalyst in my current church. (Incidentally, I was flat on my back at the time, delirious with 'flu and unable to read or listen to praise music – only pray!) Try telling me God doesn't work everything together for the good of those who love God and are called according to His purposes! He also told me that to many I would be an irritant! It was not a very nice thing to hear, but coming from the throne room of the Almighty God, who am I to argue?

If you have an irritation, you often have to give it a good scratch, which is a reaction. If just one teenager involved in destructive behaviour is triggered to think twice or consider coming back if they've lapsed then I'm comfortable to be an irritant. Anyway, none of us in the Kingdom should be surprised if we are not Mr or Mrs Popularity during the last days. Just read Jesus' words in Matthew 24:4-. He says specifically in verses 10 to 13:

> At that time many will turn away from the faith and will betray and hate each other, and many false prophets will appear and deceive many people. Because of the increase of wickedness, the love of most will grow cold, but he who stands firm to the end will be saved.

To get to the starting line does not take a grand gesture and loud prayers for you in church; it is a covenant between you and your Father. You can kneel or stand in your bedroom and say it; you can be in the supermarket queue and say it; and you can be high on alcohol and say it in a pub somewhere. The place is not important; it is your heart that matters. God sees your heart – after all, he knows what you are going to say before you even think of saying it.

Beyond the starting line? Well, that's when God really starts His work, and "what we will be has not yet been made known", but we do know that one day we shall be like Him (so the scripture says). We always have free will – God never forces us – but if we want to live in the favour of Him and are willing to be open to His guiding hand and to serve in the kingdom for His glory, through praying our way along the track, then we will be raised from one level of glory to another. How exciting is that! What better way to live is there than that? Take it from others who have had experiences spanning decades before their starting lines and have had the wisdom to listen. A simple quiet prayer is all that you need to say to start the race and a new life with Jesus.

Out of the Pigpen!

Chapter Three

How to get Born Again...

'Born again' does not mean going to church.

Don't just go to church!

Have you ever sat in church wondering how some people can manage to be happy despite their heavy workload or in spite of difficult things that they may be facing in their life? Do you find them irritating? Do you sometimes sit there thinking there must be more to this Christian life than this? Do you attend conferences and feel just like a spectator when many of your friends come back full of enthusiasm and excitement? Do you find yourself so comfortable in your life that you don't even seem to have any compassion for the less fortunate? Then you probably need to be born again. You see, since being born again I have become a completely different person. I haven't reached where God wants me to be yet – I'm definitely on a journey – but I'm on the right track!

Things could have been very different, however, if my parents hadn't moved me away from church when I was only eighteen. Had I stayed a church member, as my parents were, I could have lived my life as a churchgoer and not a fully-fledged member of the body of Christ as you become when you are born again. Jesus is coming back for his church, not for a religion. When we are just church attendees we are simply obeying a religion. However when we accept Jesus as our Lord and Saviour, confess and forsake our old life and trust him to guide us by his Spirit for the rest of our days, something amazing happens. Out with the old nature, in with the Spirit! – and the transformation begins. Without this conversion you will be left struggling in your own fleshly strength wondering what it's all about. A victorious life is what is promised for those who enter fully into the kingdom. Why not get to really know what it's all about by the power of his Spirit? Why not join the fellowship of Jesus – the family of God and the body of Christ? It doesn't matter how old you are; it's never too late to be born again. In fact Jesus commands us in John 3:3,7:

> Jesus replied, "I tell you the truth, unless you are born again you cannot see the kingdom of God ... So don't be surprised when I say 'You must be born again.'"

Church then becomes an exciting experience every week as you run to 'his house' to share testimony of a great week of blessings, or to receive prayer from your brothers and sisters if you've had a difficult time secure in the knowledge that life here couldn't be any better than this! Heaven awaits – and that's another story; an eternal future awaits you too when you accept Jesus into your heart. Interestingly, did you know that those who are not Christians can sometimes feel the presence of God and this is not a guarantee that you have been born again? We experienced this once at a Delirious concert when one of our youth group members (a non-Christian) found her arms being lifted above her head during the worship! She told us that it felt like a force was raising them up. Just imagine that same powerful force living inside of you. What are you waiting for?

To begin a new life with Jesus, please pray this prayer:

> Lord Jesus, you said you wouldn't turn away anyone who came to you.

> Jesus, I come to you now. Forgive me for having shut you out. I want to stop living life my way and start living it your way. I believe you are the Son of God. I believe you died for me and that your blood pays for my sins and provides me with the gift of eternal life.

> I believe your promises, Jesus. I receive that gift and I acknowledge you as my Lord and saviour. Amen.

It's important that you now find a church where you can be nurtured and built in as a member of the body of Christ and begin the fantastic journey to Heaven. Ask lots of questions of other more mature Christians as you go and... pray, pray, pray.

As I've studied the Bible since becoming a Christian, I've found myself understanding and identifying with many people's characters in the Good Book. For instance, how often have we 'done a Jonah' and ended up in the place where God told us to go in the first place, having done things our own way for a while? Or even 'a Peter' and denied the faith to gain approval from our friends or family?

However, if I could change places with just one person from biblical times it would be the sinful woman who ministered to Jesus in the Pharisee's house (Luke 7:36-50).

> *Therefore I tell you, her many sins have been forgiven - for she loved much. But he who has been forgiven little loves little.*

(Jesus' words about her in verse 47).

She got it! She knew who Jesus was and she also knew how amazing her life was, having received her salvation and the forgiveness of her sins. Notice how earlier Jesus used the prophetic word when dealing with the Pharisees' attitude. This example should help us in the church to understand the importance of allowing the Holy Spirit access to our innermost self so that things hidden can be revealed and brought into the wonderful light. Forgiveness is the key here. This is so that we can be free to enter into our purpose at this critical time for us as Christians. 'To love' is what is at the heart of this abundant life and only when, like the sinful woman, have we been forgiven can we fully open up and love God, others and ourselves.

Sometimes we don't even know that there is stuff to get dealt with, and sometimes we only give God the bits of our life that we choose to. Some Christians even know that there is more to life than what they are at the moment experiencing. God wants to heal all of that which is holding us back, dragging us down or hindering the flow of power from Him. It's time to use the prophetic (dreams, prophetic words and visions, healings, etc.) to defeat the enemy, not spend our time sticking to old church programmes and routines. The enemy knows our past and will use it, but the new ways that God is showing us will 'knock him into touch' so that we can all lead power-filled lives and give God glory in these last days, as well as see countless souls saved, including our friends and families.

Out of the Pigpen!

Look at the prophetic vision below (see chapter on street maps for a fuller description). We all need to be on the main road to be an army. Edifying requires us all to be in the same place, so we need to encourage each other to turn, pray, give up our confession to Him, be refilled, move forward and love. Kingdom life is free and full of God's power, glory, favour and blessings. Come in; the water's lovely!

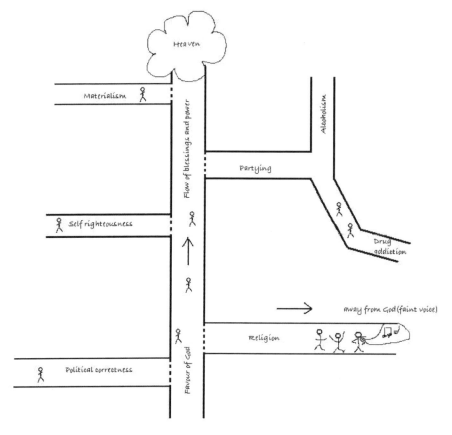

CHAPTER FOUR

God in a Box

How we put limits on God.

Common deceptions in the church today

RELIGION IS KING

Jesus didn't like religion; in fact He spoke against it several times in the Gospels. He recognised (as we must) how restrictive and rule-oriented it is. So many Christians follow a religion and don't even know that that's what they are doing and for many of us that's because it's all we've ever known. Religion has been around for a long time, and many of us have learned from a very young age to follow its rules and regulations. For example, you may be born into a family which attends church every Sunday; your parents had you christened as a baby and taught you that when you do something wrong you must kneel by your bed and say your prayers at night, or ask the priest to prescribe a number of chants for you to say to get forgiveness. If this is your experience, you don't know anything else, and you could go through your life constantly feeling that being a Christian is associated with feelings of guilt and is really not for you; so you leave church and then have a real fear of anything to do with it for the rest of your life. Unfortunately you may miss the most amazing gift that you could receive – the gift of everlasting life with Jesus, once you are born again, and the awesome power of the Holy Spirit who comes to live in you to guide and comfort you until heaven.

The enemy loves religion, and he delights in seeing bound people sitting in pews. Jesus wants you to be free. He died so that you could be free. Any church that makes up doctrine not based on God's word is deceived and is contributing to keeping many from hearing the truth. Unfortunately it's not only denominational establishments that do this. There are many free evangelical churches that also use routines and their own rules to keep people from the truth, and that can even be through teaching a diluted message just to keep people happy and attending that particular fellowship.

When you get saved and get filled with the Spirit of God then you want to be part of Jesus' body here on earth because that's what God wants. It says in the Bible that Jesus is the head, that the members of the church are the many parts of His body. It also says that we are His bride and that He will return one day for a spotless bride without wrinkles or blemishes. When you have a relationship with Jesus, He will guide you to a church and will encourage you to serve the body of Christ. That's the right way around – not being bound by a set of man-made rules of how to worship, how to conduct a service correctly, how to get your sins forgiven (till the next time).

I believe the time is coming when there will be many more Spirit-led Christians who will be able to discern through the power of God's Spirit when religious doctrine is in place. The church will once again become based on the foundation of Jesus Christ, just as it was in Acts. I can't wait!

MY PARENTS' FAITH WILL SEE ME THROUGH

Talking to kids in Sunday school, we quickly realised this deception at work in their lives. Once again the enemy has found a way of convincing Christian kids that church is boring, church is for their parents and that they are just obliged to attend out of a sense of duty. It's so sad, and it's time to deal with this honestly before more of our teenagers decide that the world has more to offer them than Jesus, and leave. We have known so many young people become so frustrated with church that they turn away completely (I was one of them, although my whole family left as I've shared in my testimony).

First of all we, as parents, have to bear some of the responsibility and demonstrate our faith by living out our lives away from church in a way that honours God. We can't be surprised if our young people turn away or are just dutiful church attendees, if that's the example we are setting. Many Christians 'do the church thing' and act 'holy' on a Sunday and then live as the rest of the world the other six days – never helping anyone, never opening their Bible and only praying when something goes wrong.

If we want our kids to be on fire for Jesus, it must start with us! When we have that sorted I believe the next step is to persuade them to be born again. You would be amazed at how many young people have not been born again and struggle with feeling bad about themselves because they feel like they are missing the mark. How can they live a fulfilling Christian life without the help of the Holy Spirit? We couldn't, so why are we surprised when they try and quite understandably fail? That's why churches with good youth ministry teams manage to help their young people in a way that many of us never quite achieve. They need a particular kind of ministry, and they need to feel valued and able to serve the church, just as the adults do. They need to talk issues through openly, without feeling insecure or condemned – being a teenager today is difficult enough without any added pressure from within the church walls. We have found the summer festivals a great source of spiritual food for our young people, but this type of input must be maintained once we get back to our own churches through prayer and provision of youth-friendly activities.

We must also teach them the absolute truth of the gospel and not be tempted to water it down or compromise to keep hold of them. The truth will set you free, whatever age you are! I have been shocked over the last few years to see some churches accepting and encouraging lifestyle choices that are totally unbiblical (and please don't think I'm judging as I teach young people myself in Sunday school), such as smoking and co-habiting whilst regularly attending church. All of us mess up, get deceived and misunderstand things, but to actually model this type of lifestyle when there are younger people coming up through the ranks is dangerous. (Remember, the Bible warns us of how quickly yeast spreads through a batch of dough). The Bible is clear that we are made righteous, but we are to live holy lives with the Holy Spirit to help us know when something is in line with God or not. These young people are being deceived and they are not being taught properly if no one tries to correct them or warn them of the consequences of their disregard of God's word.

The Bible teaches the importance of sex being within the secure relationship of marriage. Young people will not understand later how to be good parents. They may then not know how to guide their own children to make righteous decisions if they've attended a liberal church. Also, if we don't teach about addictive substances like alcohol and tobacco in the context of the Bible, which encourages us to see our bodies as temples of the Holy Spirit, then we will end up with more and more adults in church who just think it's normal to drink to excess and be addicted to a substance. If our God can do anything, even the impossible, then how is it that He can't kick a cigarette habit into touch? He can, and I can testify to that as I smoked for twenty years before being born again; but God soon sorted that out and, believe me, I had tried nicotine patches and all sorts of solutions to no effect.

The reason for the disillusionment of young church people, I believe, is the church becoming too much like the world and bowing to political correctness. We have never been told in the Bible that pleasing our children is right. Proverbs teaches, "Spare the rod; spoil the child," alongside children honouring their parents together with not frustrating our children. Nowhere does it say we must make our children happy by agreeing with any choices they make just to stay friends with them. Put like that, it's just madness not to make a stand and fight for our children to be brought up on fire for God and to encourage them to become Spirit-filled members of the kingdom in their own right as soon as possible. Otherwise, when they are no longer under our wing, how can we expect them to be able to fight off the enemy for themselves and bring up their children God's way too? That's how the kingdom will grow – not by wimping out and living in the fear of rejection by our children if we speak out for Jesus' way.

We have had to ask for prayer backup for our sixteen-year-old when he has been struggling with issues. We have great elders who always honour our prayer requests. We are bringing up our children in God's kingdom ways, so our five-year-old has never known any different. If he gets sick, he tells them at preschool that Jesus is making him better, and he always prays for his friends and relatives before even thinking of the doctors. His prayer usually goes something like, "Jesus, please make Nana better. Amen." We will keep encouraging him, but if he does come up against it we will ask for backup from our church. We believe in the power of the corporate body; when one is weak we all suffer and there is strength in interdependency.

The world will make a play for our children, but we must be ready to fight for them in an open and honest way with our fellow members of Christ's body when it does happen. Too often families hide their shame or embarrassment when a youngster gets tempted away instead of getting the army together and praying in the Spirit to break the ties on them. We are not in a competition with our fellow believers as far as our children are concerned, and if we feel that way then we haven't really 'got it' at all! Competition is of the world; co-operation is God's way. I believe that is another reason for the increase in the number of prodigals amongst our church families – the young people do not see their parents' faith as having any power at all. Even if they tell us not to embarrass them, we should not listen, because that again is a clever deception (masked as confidentiality) designed to stop corporate prayer – and prayer is where the power is. We should be getting together and honestly praying for our kids who may have fallen prey to a deception (usually due to immaturity); why else do we have faith if not to fight for our precious children? God gave His Son for us, yet we are too proud to just open ourselves up to a little temporary embarrassment for ours. It's all about trusting each other, that when we are weak, others are strong. Trials come to all of us, but we are placed in a body of believers so that we can carry each other's burdens when going it alone seems too much.

We must be seen by our children to be doers of the word, or they will not see faith as important enough to stand on. We must become radical parents if we are to see a wave of youngsters reviving the nation with God's ways. We have to feed them and teach them the right way – believing in God's word above everything else, regardless of what the world does or says. Only then will they be able to come back to the Father's house, when they've finished their wanderings, knowing that the foundation and truths are waiting solidly for them. We must be loving, obedient followers if we want our kids to be healthy, successful leaders in the future society where God will be at the centre of life and where I believe every knee will bow to Jesus.

THIS IS THE WAY WE DO CHURCH

Another way we put God in a box is to insist on creating a church which is consumer oriented. Once we've got the fish in the aquarium we feel we need to make it so comfortable that they will never want to leave! We create a place where we have our favourite worship style week in week out and where the people who attend come to consume whatever is on offer. We have a beautiful building and sometimes the ideology that we need to please people to keep them in the pews of our church. A healthy church stays aligned to God's plan and is never afraid to change; it finds out what God wants to do. When we become part of the body of Christ we need to look for ways of using our talents and 'giftings' to serve our church community, not look for what we can get out of the worship or the teaching (although of course that is intended for us to grow). It's amazing just how prevalent church-hopping is at the present time, where members move to several different fellowships each year because someone has upset them. (Remember the Israelites in the desert moaning and complaining even though they were fed and watered supernaturally). This is absolutely not what God intended when He created it this way. I believe we are put into a church specifically to do a job predestined for us. We may end up being with someone whom we would never choose as a friend but who causes us to grow in character far more than we would have believed possible. Again this 'hopping' comes out of our culture of choice and pleasure, where we feel we must be allowed to select the experiences that give us the greatest buzz or satisfaction. That again is a deception, and as long as we keep hopping, the enemy is happy because we then never truly find out our purpose in the body and therefore we never really make much of an impact for the kingdom. I'm not saying that God never moves us, because He can do what He pleases and I know many obedient men and women of God who have been moved around a lot by God and have produced some great fruit for the kingdom because that was their calling.

When we go to church I believe we should be there to be a blessing, to be faithful and to serve as Jesus did with the disciples (as

He so brilliantly demonstrated when He washed their feet). We have so many overworked pastors in our churches that it's time for us to offer our services to them. As the Bible says, "Present yourselves as living sacrifices." Jesus is coming back for a spotless bride, so anything we can do to help that process, rather than demanding we get fed and watered until we can hardly move with knowledge, the better. Even if you can only make tea, you can make tea for Jesus. Even if you can only garden, you can garden for Jesus – and usually that one thing that you are good at and enjoy, God wants to use to serve your community. After all, unless we get out of our buildings many people will not get to see faith in action or hear the good news of the gospel. Initiatives like street pastors are successful because the outside world sees that faith means something, and that is how people will become interested in hearing about Jesus and accept Him for themselves as their personal Saviour.

I JUST DIDN'T KNOW THAT (IGNORANCE IS BLISS)

God knows our hearts, He knows our minds, He knows our motives, and He knows everything about us; so when people claim that they were unaware of a particular truth it is often a lie to cover up sin. I'd just like to make a distinction here to clarify this deception in case you are worried that on the day of judgement God will 'tackle you' about something you really never knew about. My Dad was a member of the Methodist church, but he rarely attended and he certainly never lived a Spirit-filled life until right at the end. The point is he never knew any different, and God only holds us accountable for what we know, I believe. However, to feign ignorance when you are part of a born-again church where the teaching is sound is not going to excuse anyone on the day of judgement for those who have chosen to disobey or ignore God. The Bible says we will escape as one going through fire; what that means I for one don't really want to find out. I would prefer to be in the camp who hears those amazing words, "Well done, good and faithful servant."

So, this is a heart matter and a very real deception in Christian life today. For example if you hear someone teach on the importance of being born again (because Jesus said it is necessary for all believers) and yet during the altar call you still don't give your life to Jesus you cannot later claim that you didn't know. You see, my Dad never attended such a service, so in his heart he didn't know that was so, but if someone knows it but doesn't do it, what do we call that? It could be doubt, it could be disobedience, it could be unbelief; nevertheless that's just one aspect of Christian teaching that people think is an 'opt in or opt out' matter! There is only one gospel (one foundation), and it's time we began to think carefully in our different denominations and fellowships what we are building for the future because what Christians believe should always be what is written in the word and nothing else.

Therefore, put simply, we should all have the same beliefs – we are called to one faith, one baptism – and that is why it's so important that everyone studies the Bible for themselves and that everyone has a prayer life and does not become dependent on a pastor feeding them. When I get a chance to chat with my Dad in heaven I will be able to ask him what happened when I prayed for him when he was on life support and how great it was to be born again (see section entitled 'More to come').

Studying an area we are unsure of always brings clarity – just as it did when we were growing in the area of tithing. At first my husband and I were unsure of what to do, but when we looked up all the scriptures in that area we got information, truth and revelation about how to manage our finances in line with God. Now we know, God knows we know, so if we decided to not tithe ten percent of our income then we could be held accountable for that decision! Usually, however, once you have studied the area in God's word and you know the truth you would never want to go back to ignorance, so it's true that 'the truth will set you free' (even if you think ignorance is bliss). God always looks at your heart.

"WHY CAN'T IT BE LIKE THE OLD DAYS?"

It's amazing how many times I've heard people in churches talk about how they wish it could be like the 'old days'. That is so sad; the truth is we can never – and should never – go back to how things were in the past because God does everything at the right time for our own good. Remember again the Israelites wishing that they could go back to Egypt! Why? – when it was in Egypt that they were kept as slaves. I've even seen Christians trying to recreate some kind of 'revisiting of days gone' by through worship, service content and delivering outdated lessons. Whilst it is very healthy to remember God's goodness to us back then and even recount past miracles in the context of thankfulness and encouragement, it is dangerous to say the old days were better. It is just not biblically correct, and it is based on feelings. Furthermore, if we say the 'old days' were better we are actually saying that we haven't grown at all or that we have gone backwards! The Bible talks about the Christian going from one level of glory to another, which means that the level we are at now is higher than in our past (otherwise we may not actually be in God at all). God designs our walk with Him to help us to develop our character to be more like Jesus, so ten years ago we were less like Jesus than we are today (if we have stuck with God and allowed him to mould and shape us).

The problem here is that some people look back and either realise suddenly that they are further away from God than they were previously or they haven't grown at all. They also may have had many trials in the current season of their life and begun to moan and complain and wish for times past when things were good. The Bible tells us to press on – we will have trials, but we always know that God will be with us through them. If our characters have grown to a new level of glory and we have become more mature in how we handle situations, we should be more in line with God's way by now. Therefore what we go through today will not seem as difficult as in the past when we were more immature and less like Jesus.

When I consider my Mum dying twelve years ago and I remember my reactions to her death (this was before I was born again) it shocks me. I was angry; I was terrible to live with, and I lashed out at my Dad when he got a new partner, and so on. If I compare myself then to the 'me' who had to cope with Dad dying very recently, I could see the difference. I had the peace and comfort of the Holy Spirit with me throughout this difficult time, and that is hard to even describe. The Bible talks about it being a peace beyond understanding and that it is perfect peace in the middle of the trouble.

Troubles will be here all the time we are on the earth, but the closer our relationship with God the less distressing they will be. Regrets from the past can also be damaging, and so it's important to keep moving forward whilst learning the lesson from darker days. We can make ourselves not look backwards by quoting scriptures that fix our minds on us being 'not where we have come from but not yet where we will be' at the end of our journey. I want to keep pressing on towards the finish line, working with God through the conviction of the Holy Spirit, so that I can move up to the next level of glory and see many more people come to know Him and begin their journey of growth.

Don't be like the Israelites who took forty years to make an eleven-day trip because of their murmuring and complaining; have a mindset that agrees to work *with* God rather than fight His plan for you. How many people give up just before their breakthrough? And how many people die in the wilderness? We just end up going around the same mountain until we 'get it'. I believe God doesn't move us on until we have got whatever He is trying to push us through, whether it is unforgiveness, fearfulness, stubborn sins, or whatever.

We are all different, but God knows exactly what we need. Don't look back! What was necessary then (and what is now) is exactly what was needed to take you onwards and upwards to the higher level. This time next year we should be able to look back and see just how God has changed us for the better; we may be less angry or more patient, or we may be more loving or less judgemental. Here's to enjoying the journey!

GOD DOESN'T DO THAT

How many times have you heard someone put limits on God by saying that He wouldn't 'do this or that' or "That that's not how God works" or "I don't believe God is like that"? The truth is that if we really know God we quickly realise that because God is God, He can do absolutely anything, "immeasurably more than we can ever hope or imagine"[1]. Usually these sweeping statements about Him come out of our mouths when we are struggling to explain why something didn't turn out how we hoped and prayed it would or when we want to do something that clearly is opposite to what the Bible says.

For example, when we have prayed for someone who is sick and they don't recover, we begin to try and make sense of it; we may try to blame someone or some circumstance not being quite right so it

---

[1] Ephesians 3:20

didn't happen. That's just reducing God down to a formula, which is not right. God alone knows why some people get healed and others go on to the next chapter of their life, which is eternal. We must only listen and do our part during that time, so that what we actually can say truthfully is "I trust God. I did all I was asked to do, and I know that God will make all things work together for the good of those who are called according to His purpose."

It's usually when we have said no to something that God has asked us to do, during that painful time, that excuses, regrets and guilt can plague our mind. That's why obedience to God is essential in our Christian life. However strange the instruction may be from God, it is important to follow it, whatever the final outcome. We must have confidence that he has given us the wisdom and discernment to hear his voice and truly know it's a word from him, so there is no reason to doubt. During my dad's time on life support, an elder of our church received a word from God – that we should pray over a towel and that I was to place it on Dad when I went to visit. I did this in obedience, even though those words, "God wouldn't do this," were on the tip of my tongue. As I did this and prayed for him, the colour came into his cheeks and his eyelids flickered. Who knows what was happening in the spirit, but it was all good. So obedience is everything. Even though it was, I believe, his time to die (we all have one), he had a great send-off.

Also, I've heard Christians say that God wasn't telling them to give up smoking or drinking right now! If you remember that the gospel is all about freedom, why would someone say that God wanted to keep him or her bound in addiction? Because they wanted to continue sinning! I've heard homosexuality, co-habitation, depression, and alcoholism all justified by Christians. We have to stop it, because apart from the damage it does to our relationship with Father God, and apart from the fact that it will come up at judgement day, is the harm it does the unsaved. Why would they want to step out in faith to accept Jesus when they see it has made no difference whatsoever to those who profess to be born again? They see no difference between us and the people of this world if we classify God as being able to only do 'this or that'. I believe everything is possible and nothing is impossible with God, so I have set my mind to obey, then I absolutely know I'll have no regrets.

Out of the Pigpen!

I DON'T DESERVE IT; MY FAMILY IS A MESS!

When you become a Christian by being born into God's family, you are a new creation. You no longer belong to the world; you now have the potential, due to the new life that has been put inside of you, to be a victorious member of God's body on the earth where Jesus is the head. However, many of us never think like that; we end up tied to our family history by thoughts in our mind that hold us back from inheriting the life which God intended for us when we were born again. For instance, you may have had an earthly father who was a strict disciplinarian and whose love for you was very much conditional on you behaving correctly. You may have been physically abused or emotionally harmed by stuff from your childhood or dysfunctional relationships as an adult. We can then tend to see Father God in terms of what we know an earthly father to be from our own experiences. We may think that God is therefore harsh or distant. We need to shift our minds and bring our thoughts about us in line with God's thoughts about us. God is love; His love for us is unconditional; He loves us with an everlasting love and His grace means that forgiveness, not performance, is the key to a healthy relationship with him.

Absolutely anything can be healed from our past as long as we open the door for God to work and believe his word. He will only come into that secret place by invitation – we must trust him and believe that he can do the impossible. Sometimes this can be a gradual process of growing and changing under the guidance of the precious Holy Spirit. We must stay connected for this to happen in our lives, or reconnect if we have become disconnected for whatever reason. The enemy is a master at disconnecting Christians from God and planting justification for wrong thinking or doubts about worthiness into the mind. 2 Corinthians 10:4-5 explains what we must do as sons and daughters of the living God when this happens.

> For the weapons of our warfare are not carnal but mighty in God for pulling down strongholds, casting down arguments and every high thing that exalts itself against the knowledge of God, bringing every thought into captivity to the obedience of Christ, and being ready to punish all disobedience when your obedience is fulfilled. (KJV)

Praying that God would cut off the ties to the past can bring down most strongholds that exist in our minds. This may mean you need to pray with another person or a group of people whom you trust and who will stand with you. We have seen people completely set free of their troubled past through this kind of prayer, and it is during this time that God may prompt you to forgive someone (such as an earthly father or an abusive husband) who may have caused your way of thinking in the first place. You may have had a bad start in life, but you can have a fantastic finish. When the enemy begins to niggle at you after you have been set free (which he will – that's his style) you must intentionally cast down in Jesus' name what he whispers. If you make up your mind, he will leave you and move to someone who is not yet fully convinced of their place in God's family. It's about knowing, finally, who your real Father is and living by the rules of heaven not earth. There is no need for any of us sons and daughters to remain bound by the past, whatever happened there. God is not shocked by any of it; he knows all about it, and he knows exactly what each of us needs to set us free, but it is dependent on us trusting him to help us through a relationship with him. Learn to listen to His voice and shut out the voice of the enemy. Remember, one builds you up, the other tears you down. Father God wants you to walk with him through every one of your days here on the earth, and that's how we will live victorious, free and happy lives – lives of which others will begin to ask, "What's your secret? Why are you always so happy and peaceful?" You know the rest of the story, as it's already written in the Bible: many more people will come to know Him through the church, which will be a light on a hill. What an exciting time to be alive! Don't waste a second of it because once you get to heaven you won't be able to make a difference. Now is the time! So...

- Be born again as young as possible.
- Take responsibility for your own walk with God.
- Tell the truth and only believe the truth of the word.
- Fight for those who are struggling with God's weapons of love and prayer.
- Serve your church and be a blessing.
- Study the Bible and learn.

Out of the Pigpen!

- Don't look back; press on to the finish.
- Listen and obey. God can and will do anything. Trust Him.

Chapter Five

People-Pleasing

Pleasing God is the only way to truly please people.

When we live our lives trying to please people we end up feeling frustrated and unfulfilled as a Christian, and the really sad thing is that when we get caught in this trap we also end up not pleasing God. We have to compromise our beliefs to keep others happy, and that often means that we don't honour God and we may only even be obedient to certain parts of the Bible and unfortunately disobedient to much of what God says. However, when we make up our minds that we are going to please God whatever the cost, then curiously we end up pleasing people anyway because we haven't compromised our faith. The uncompromisingly righteous Christian life is not only more fulfilling, but it is also more powerful because it is when you are obedient to God that you experience the blessings and favour which accompany it.

There are many different types of people-pleasing in the world today to watch out for. (Sometimes we need someone to point it out before we even recognise its existence in us.)

- Pleasing yourself
- Pleasing your family
- Pleasing a non-Christian partner or spouse
- Pleasing friends
- Pleasing your employer
- Pleasing society (materialism, political correctness, corruption)

Out of the Pigpen!

Just look at Noah, Joseph and Daniel as examples of lives that pleased God. As they went about their lives, serving God and honouring Him above people, they received blessings and favour beyond their wildest dreams. What would have happened if these men had been people-pleasers? I can't imagine life was too great for Noah's wife and children as he set about building the ark. I'm sure he was nagged a few times to spend more time with the family, but the point is he didn't compromise and his family was saved along with him because he stuck with God and he obeyed God's will for his life. It was God's will that he should save the human race and he did it. So I'm sure his wife and children appreciated his sacrifice in the end.

Similarly if Joseph had been persuaded to please his brothers or Potipher's wife then, although he would have been possibly spared some of the difficult times in his life, he would not have born the fruit for God that he did.

Likewise, if Daniel had bowed down to the king just to please him, then he wouldn't have been able to bless Nebuchadnezzar and others by interpreting their dreams and visions (his God-given calling). Ultimately, he wouldn't have been so trusted by God to reveal the end time prophesies at the end of his life or have been supernaturally protected from the jaws of the lions.

Of course, there are many more examples of people in the Bible who dedicated their lives to pleasing God and there is no better example than Jesus who so wonderfully demonstrated a life of honouring His Father even unto death.

PLEASING YOURSELF

This is by far the easiest deception to fall for because the society we live in is always telling us through the media that we have free choice. Because of this, it's just so natural for us to live our lives consuming what our culture is offering without really thinking about it. Teenagers, in particular, tend to think that it is normal to walk around with headphones in their ears listening to whatever is the latest chart hit banging in their ears. They think nothing of sitting for hours on end communicating via the internet or Facebook with their friends or walking along with a mobile phone attached to the side of their head. Violent computer games fill much of the spare time of young lads, whilst shopping can be a marathon event for teenage girls. I'm not being a killjoy, as I too like picking up a new skirt or jacket, particularly if it's in the sale and a real bargain (but that's probably an age thing). However, what is sad is that this becomes a lifestyle choice for many, not just a pastime. Unfortunately this lifestyle can become more addictive and all-consuming, and God can simply be put in a box reserved just for Sunday morning. People live for what pleases them most of the week and only turn their minds to even thinking about God when it's time for a church meeting.

Jonah was a perfect example of someone who pleased himself, but it was pointless for him to ignore God. Jonah 1:1 says:

> The word of the Lord came to Jonah son of Amittai: "Go to the great city of Nineveh and preach against it, because its wickedness has come up before me." But Jonah ran away from the Lord and headed for Tarshish.

We know the rest of the story, as a big fish swallowed Jonah; he was taught by God and ended up where God wanted him to be all along.

Deep down we know that God has great plans and purposes for us, but we choose (often by deception) to go our own way because we think we can 'have it all'. The Bible teaches us that we must lose our life to gain it and that we need to give ourself as a living sacrifice. You have no idea, until you go for it, how liberating and exciting a life really lived for God can be. Set your mind so that when God tells you to do something (and He wants to use every single one of us, whatever our age or experience) that you simply say, "Yes!" and just ask, "How quickly?" I believe God always honours a life dedicated to serving Him; so although it is tempting to want the stuff of this world, as He knows the desires of our heart he quite often blesses us by giving them to us anyway! I don't pretend to understand this principle but the Bible does say, "Seek first the kingdom and the rest will be given to you."

Start today and just try to think of how much time you spend with God and how much time you spend on yourself; it's a great way of seeing whether you are pleasing yourself or not. This was quite a shock for me, and I had to prayerfully make more than a few adjustments to my daily schedule. Our mindset is critical here, as we can devote our working lives to serving God using our 'giftings' to bless people at work or we can see our employment as a way of getting money to get more stuff, when most of us have already got more than enough stuff. Pray about this and, believe me, God is waiting and wanting to bless you! Also, as we change our mind to be more in line with God, we don't even want the things of the world anymore. We actually would rather spend time praying or worshipping in preference to playing computer games or watching TV as that is what we need to do to stay close to God.

PLEASING YOUR FAMILY

Sometimes we can slip into thinking that by doing what our family want us to do (as opposed to what God wants us to do) is right, when actually it is damaging both to us and to those members of our family who are not yet saved. For example, when our children are having a time in their lives when they are questioning their faith and begin to experiment with things of the world it is very easy to bow to the pressure of spending time with them doing secular activities instead of doing what we know in our heart is pleasing to God. This is all about balance, of course, as there are going to be times when it is definitely right to miss a church meeting to spend time with our family. It's all about relationship with our Father. He will tell us what to do for the best if we remember to ask Him (after all, prayer is simply talking to God). They may then think that our faith is really not that important to us either and can become subconsciously even more discouraged.

Sadly I have had to lose contact with some members of my family who put pressure on me to agree with really corrupt actions. When I had to fight for what I believed was right according to my beliefs (the relatives mentioned are not Christians) and rejected their way of doing things with regards my dad's estate, they decided not to keep in touch with me. I could not compromise my beliefs in this instance and it has meant temporarily not seeing some members of my family. However, I pray for them all the time, and I trust that in God's timing it will all be put right. Because my husband and I have set our minds on pleasing God, I believe that they will one day come to know Him too in His perfect timing. Keeping that connection with God is the most important thing in our life and reminds me of when Jesus said in the Gospels, "Who is my mother and who are my brothers? Those who do the will of my Father."[2] So we inherit spiritual brothers and sisters, but it may mean that as we grow closer to God we may get further away from our earthly brothers and sisters. As the Bible tells us that one day every knee will bow to Jesus, it's worth sticking to His promises, as we will have a long time in eternity to smooth things over with them, even if they sometimes don't understand us now. The key for us here is to keep on praying for them and never give up; one day God will give us the right time and even the right words to speak to them, and that could be when they have nowhere else to turn. Our prayers can only be effective when we are living God's way, so if we do succumb to doing what they want us to do our prayers will be ineffective. Read James if you want to see why double-mindedness is a bad idea!

If we bow to the pressure now to please them, we may have to dishonour God – and that is counterproductive. Everyone wants to be in contact with members of their family, but we need to understand that if we are pushed to make a choice between God and them, both for our sake and for theirs we must always choose God. He is a God of restoration so we must trust that He will do what's best for us always and listen carefully in what can be times of trouble. Writing a letter to explain what you believe and why you can't do what your family may ask you to do is a good way of avoiding confrontational conversations which won't help anybody. Above all, we should never try to please both God and our family, watering down what we believe, but always speak the truth as sensitively as we are able and most importantly, pray, pray, pray!

PLEASING A NON-CHRISTIAN SPOUSE

I heard someone preach once that we should be like thermostats not like thermometers, and nowhere is that more important than in a relationship where one person is a Christian and the other is not. Similarly it is also true for a couple where one person is a member of a liberal church and the other a member of a Bible-believing one. (How sad is it, incidentally, that even amongst churches we can have radically different beliefs!) Jesus said, "I am the way and the truth

---

[2] Matthew 12:48

and the life,"[3] so there is only one way to truly live and that is believing all of God's word, not just the bits we like! To be a thermostat you change the climate around you, but when you are a thermometer you simply reflect the atmosphere around you. One way changes people to be more like you; the other way changes you to be more like those around you. The Bible says that we are to spread the word so that more people can come to know Him, so it's very clear which one we are supposed to be to please God.

It must be so hard for a Christian to stay strong when they are married to a non-Christian, as it's often difficult to get to church every week due to your husband or wife wanting to share time together. As the membership in the body of Christ is so important right now because of the covenant relationship between us and God and between each other, that could mean that it becomes difficult to serve the body regularly and you may miss important teaching or fellowship. This is all about balance; sometimes it is necessary to miss meetings and not become legalistic, as the Christian life should be about living the gospel seven days a week, not just for an hour on a Sunday!

The critical point here is that if our spouse is going to also become a Christian, they should see our faith as important to us, not just a club we go to meet people, although as has already been mentioned the relationships between our brothers and sisters are crucial for the interdependency that God designed the church to exhibit. When we demonstrate that sacrificial commitment, difficult as it may be in this type of relationship, our spouse is more likely to want to join us. I remember when I met my now husband. He was a born-again Christian and I wasn't. He continued in His church commitments, attending meetings and organising the sound for the worship on a Sunday. It wasn't long before I was going to home group with him and hearing about Jesus for myself. The rest is history, as it didn't take long for me to commit to becoming a Christian and getting baptised in a river, all within a very short space of time. We now serve our church together as well as supporting each other with prayer and joint Bible reading and having our own times spent with God.

---

[3] John 14:6

Life could have been so different for both of us if he had become a thermometer and not stuck to being a thermostat! How often do Christians go out with a non-believer and drop all things to do with church, not even mentioning Jesus anymore? Pretty soon they are having a physical relationship, then living together and acting just like any unsaved couple. Is that pleasing God? Sadly many people justify all wrong actions by saying that God's grace will cover them. That is very definitely twisting the truth to suit us, I believe, in order to carry on pleasing our partner. It takes a lot of determination and prayer to stay on the right track but, as I hope I've shown, it's critical for a healthy, honourable relationship with Father God and also imperative if our husband or wife is to follow our example and have the best life possible for them too! I'm so thankful for the husband I have, and just maybe he was sent by God to guide me to Him. You too can do that if you'll only stick to your guns.

PLEASING FRIENDS

Anyone who has children will be all too familiar with their son or daughter coming out with the line, "Mum, can I go to this party?" As we have a sixteen-year-old son it's something we hear all the time. Unfortunately more often than not the answer has to be no, because parties today often involve the heavy use of alcohol or worse (sometimes purchased by liberal parents or older siblings). This does not make us popular; as parents and we seem to have to have quite a few discussions about what can happen at these events. We try to explain that if he simply goes along pleasing his friends to be popular (he's a popular lad anyway so that helps), he may struggle to avoid temptation until he's a bit older!

Peer pressure is very powerful and we all want to belong and feel accepted, but I believe that whatever age we are we can avoid the pitfalls of this as long as we aim to please God. When we become a Christian we are part of His family. We are His sons and daughters and co-heirs with Jesus. As long as we stay focussed on Him and really let the promises of our inheritance sink deep into us then it is more difficult to become deceived by peer pressure. Deception is subtle and persuasive, but providing we are connected to God in close relationship with Him, then the Holy Spirit will warn us if something is not good for us. It's simply like having a highly tuned conscience.

Out of the Pigpen!

Have you ever stopped to think what religion is? It's simply an extreme form of people-pleasing. When we devise a set of procedures to follow or schedule church by the clock or by orders of service, we are keeping control. We go to a place where we all like the same kind of music or person teaching, and often the format never changes because to keep the same people in the pews each week we have to please them. God often blows a wind of change through churches, and I believe we are about to see things alter amongst our fellowships. The really successful churches (those that bring in the lost) in these times will be those who do please God and who do not try to keep a tight control of the Spirit moving. The point is, God is waiting to bless churches with growth; we just need to tune in more closely to His will and listen and obey like we never have before. It will be brilliant to see those beacons of God's righteousness shining all around the world, run by teams of willing pairs of hands reaching out to the communities around them.

PLEASING YOUR EMPLOYER

I heard a story only recently of a gas engineer who left his Palm Sunday cross on the dashboard of his vehicle as a witness to his Christian beliefs. Needless to say, along with countless other employees all over our country who have been asked to take off their cross necklaces, he was told to remove it from view by his employer. He faced the sack from his job if he didn't conform. What do you do in those circumstances? Do you please God and stay true to your beliefs, or do you please your employer and not show the cross? It doesn't mean you believe any less, but it does take away a good evangelistic opportunity to respond to questions about your choices.

Jesus told us before He died that we would be persecuted and hated because of Him, and compared to people in other parts of the world who can be killed for believing in Jesus we are relatively free in the west. Each person needs to pray and ask God what to do whenever situations like this arise in our lives, and that's how our relationship with Him grows and our character too. I have never been asked to remove my cross when I've been at work, and I've had many opportunities to talk to my colleagues about my beliefs.

I believe in being open to any opportunity to pray for people, talk to them about Jesus or do church missions work, as I think this is in line with what God wants us to do on the earth in these days. When others see we are different and we stand up for what we believe with confidence then I think they see it as something worth thinking about themselves. If it pleases God then we should do it, and if we lose our job then I'm sure we will be blessed with a better one because we have acted obediently to His call on our lives. I don't think, however we should be confrontational and rude as that is definitely not Biblical. We are told to obey the law of the land and also to work for our employer (however harsh) as though we were working for God. It's a difficult area, but crucially our relationship with God has to come first in our lives and if we get that right the rest will fall into place. We've always found that changes in our employment have been timely and for a reason maybe not known at the time but always for our benefit.

PLEASING OUR CULTURE

Does the culture you live in matter when you are a Christian? When you live in a part of the world where it is outlawed to believe in Jesus then it very much matters, and we have all heard about those dear people who have died rather than deny Jesus. But what about in a corrupt culture or in a materialistic one?

I remember once writing a piece for a book about the Jesus culture, which made me think a lot about how to avoid the cultural deceptions that we live in. In this culture in which we live, independence is king, so the enemy will use that against us! We are encouraged to build our little empires, whether based on our family or our business, and many people spend their whole lives striving to keep their company on top or to keep all the members of their family in the manner to which they have become accustomed. As we are also a very materialistic society, it's important to have a nice house, car, maybe a couple of holidays a year and put our children through university and beyond! The list is endless, and usually we end up stressed, overworked, sometimes alcohol-dependent and certainly not happy if we live by Western society's rules. As a Christian we sometimes end up living a double life which can involve going to church and praying and reading sometimes but living just like our unsaved friends and relatives the rest of the time. We cannot expect to receive the same level of victory or protection as someone who lives Christianity as a lifestyle. In other words we are called to give up our life to serve God and the church so that others will see our light and want it for themselves too. We are meant to be different; we are special and we should celebrate and honour that privilege of our inheritance as sons and daughters by growing in our faith and becoming more holy and more like Jesus, as we continue forward by staying close to Him.

Believe me, people are tired of striving in a materialistic, corrupt or poverty-stricken society and they are looking for a way out (a solution); we need to remember that *we are it!* We are God's plan for the world. We are the city on the hill. That's why we are put into groups of other Christians in churches, to increase the power and prepare the bride for His return. Unfortunately we have tended to build an ineffective church culture which has been very insular and at times self-righteous; this has turned people away, not drawn them to us. We need to turn from that now and get into His plan for the world and do our little bit for Him, whichever church we are placed in.

When we realise that we can be the Jesus culture (part of His body in the earth with Jesus as the Head) then life feels right. Only recently our five-year-old was experiencing breathing difficulties, so we prayed and spoke words over him. When we sensed that he wasn't improving we used our prayer line which our church has set up. As soon as I had called one of our leaders with our prayer request (as naturally we felt a bit weak when Jude couldn't breathe), she set off the chain of others praying for him. I felt so lifted as we went to hospital with him, knowing that we had backup even as we fought to keep him awake in the back of the car all the way there. The scripture that I kept saying over and over was, "He that is in you is greater than he that is in the world." You see, our culture is independent, whereas the Jesus culture is interdependent. The Bible says that when one suffers we all suffer, when one is weak others are strong; so it makes sense to call on one another.

This week it was us who needed help, but there have been occasions when we have helped others in our church family when they have been struggling. There is power in corporate prayer. I don't understand it and I'm not meant to, but we must get over our worldly urge to keep our stuff private and fight against competition and pride, because they are tactics by the enemy to keep us from victory. I believe that because many people loved Jude and humbled themselves before God and prayed for him, he was healed up quickly and we could praise God for a great victory for His glory. As we watched his oxygen levels go up from the eighties to one hundred percent within the day we knew our brothers and sisters were praying.

Cooperation is God's will for us, and through that we learn to love and know Him more. We also learn to love and trust each other more as we support one other through the trials and troubles that the Bible tells us we will have as long as we live here on the earth. However, we also know that when this life is over we will live an eternal one with Jesus so it makes sense to live to please Him and do things His way while we are here, because that is the only way to live in the stream of blessings and power He has designed for those who live to love and serve Him. There are victories here so there is no need to live feeling defeated, tired, stressed and so on just like the rest of those in our culture; otherwise why did Jesus die? He died so that you could have life in abundance.

We do have a free will, given by God, so we need to choose to please Him rather than ourselves, our family or our culture. Don't forget, we are not doing this alone; we have the awesome Holy Spirit placed inside us to comfort and guide us. But we must remember to go to Him in prayer through all of our lives, whether we are in the middle of good times or bad, as then we have maintained the connection which gives us that peace beyond all understanding that Jesus talks about in the Bible, whatever we may go through.

So, pray today that you may learn by the power of His Spirit to be a God-pleaser not a people-pleaser. When you do that people will be drawn to you and you will end up being a *genuine* people-pleaser as you lead them to real life through Jesus. Genuine faith is the only thing that Satan is frightened of, so work with the Holy Spirit to develop that real heartfelt, unselfish devotion to Him and others that will send the enemy running and bring in more victories for His glory. Think about it; how can there be victories without trials?

What pleases God?

- When we know we are loved by Him
- When we allow Him to change and mould us into His ways

Out of the Pigpen!

- When we know we are His children and obey because we love Him
- When we worship Him in Spirit and in truth
- When we serve His church willingly (including tithing)
- When we love others and ourselves as He does
- When we help others as Jesus did
- When we stay faithful and honour His word above anything the world has to offer even when times are tough
- When we tell others about Him and give Him glory
- When we pray and intercede for others

How many more can you think of?

What does the Bible say about pleasing God?

1 John 2:17 (NLT)
And this world is fading away along with everything that people crave. But anyone who does what pleases God will live forever.

1 John 5:14 (NLT)
And we are confident that He hears us whenever we ask for anything that pleases Him.

Ephesians 5:10 (AMP)
And try to learn (in your experience), What is pleasing to the Lord (let your lives be constant proofs of what is most acceptable to Him).

Philippians 2:13 (NLT)
For God is working in you, giving you the desire and power to do what pleases Him.

1 Timothy 2:1-4 (NLT)
I urge you, first of all, to pray for all people. Ask God to help them, intercede on their behalf, and give thanks for them. Pray this way for kings and all who are in authority so that we can live peaceful and quiet lives marked by godliness and dignity. This is good and pleases God our Saviour who wants everyone to be saved and to understand the truth.

1 Peter 4:19 (NLT)
So, if you are suffering in a manner that pleases God, keep on doing what is right, and trust your lives to the God who created you, for He will never fail you.

CHAPTER SIX

The Journey of the Christian

Here on earth: how to clear out the blockages and live above the earth.

The journey of the Christian life

Christian life is often described in the Bible as a walk, a journey, a race or battle – all active words – not doubting the fact that we all need stillness and quiet times. (Jesus always prayed in between action, often alone, sometimes with others.)

GOD THE CREATOR

God is described in the Bible as creator, author, builder, and gardener. The heavens were empty until He spoke all of creation into being. A page is blank until the author writes the first word; a plot of land is bare until the first foundation stone is laid; and a field or garden is barren until seeds have been sown and the land cultivated. What happens when you try to write on a page that has something already written on it, or try to build a house on a site that is already occupied, or try to grow a field of corn or a beautiful border of flowers on a patch of weeds? They all have to be cleared first, or all that is produced is a mixed-up mess. We need to be so open and trusting in God's knowledge and care of us as His son or daughter that we allow ourself to be changed and moulded into what He wants us to be, through the conviction of the Holy Spirit. If we take on a persona, created by a combination of this world and church rituals, then we become just like the field of weeds or the crowded building plot. In other words we can't be used by God – an agent of His Spirit and an ambassador for Him – unless we allow Him first to clear our fields, unblock our wells or remove the hard places from our hearts which have been built up, almost without us noticing, over the years. To be born again is an amazing experience, and maybe it's time for the Christians who have been in pews for a very long time to undergo this transformation so that the bride can really start to get ready for His return.

The kingdom of Heaven is attainable, reachable, and accessible to all of us who believe, if we choose to stick to what God says in His word.

Revelation 12:10 talks of Satan being cast down and all power and authority being here from that point.

> *Now have come the salvation and the power and the kingdom of*
> *our God, and the authority of his Christ.*
> *For the accuser of our brothers,*
> *Who accuses them before our God day and night,*
> *Has been hurled down.*

Where did Satan end up? On the earth. What is his mission? To cause as much trouble as possible and to rule the earth. However, we are not of this world. We are in the kingdom of Heaven, which is above the earth. So we will have power and authority when we have cast down the enemy in our own lives. We have a choice: to stay in the kingdom (it is safe there) or 'click into' this world where Satan is. When we are strong in our own identity in God, trips to earth are no trouble at all. But when we participate in the things of this world, we have no power because we have joined the opposition. To make a difference, we must be in the kingdom of Heaven when we walk on the earth.

We do experience this (in church when we are worshipping and the Holy Spirit comes down or when we spend time with God, reading or praying at home). But success will come (miracles and blessings) when we do our everyday things whilst still at His feet. Why leave that place? Others will see it, just like the light that is in us. Why turn our light out when we are doing our ordinary things? Keep it on to maintain power and authority.

CHAPTER SEVEN

From One Level of Glory to Another

How to move between levels of glory. Order of success in Christian life: a step-by-step guide to living with heavenly authority.

Order of success in Christian life

1. TURN (SAME AS 'REPENT' – CHANGE OF MINDSET)

    Remember, He is looking for you.

    As in the story of the prodigal son, God is looking for you in the distance, waiting with bated breath for you to glance over your shoulder and say, "I'm ready now to change."

2. LISTEN, AS A CHILD OF GOD.

    Listen attentively; wait at His feet (Martha vs. Mary). Take His advice / instruction for as long as it takes to receive healing. During the IHOP outpouring in the USA, meetings have lasted as long as fifteen hours, with people praying, praising and receiving healing.

3. PRESENCE

    When you go about your business, stay at his feet. Take the thought of sitting there with you into the world, and always stay tuned in to the Holy Spirit. When He prompts you to witness you will be able and ready to really do it, sincerely preaching (telling the good news). The closer you are to Him the more others will see it too, as there will be something different about you. They will seek your favour, advice and company.

4. WARFARE.

When you meet the devil – tapping at first, whispering words of doubt, unbelief, and confidence-sapping murmurings – one word will see him off. "In the name of Jesus, go!" As long as you are in God and God is in you. If you're intentionally sinning, you might need help to get rid of a stronghold. (See the lesson on 'God is our Father'.)

Don't get isolated; get backup from other members of the body.

5. MINISTRY/GIFTING

God may give you a word for your church, friend or family member, or even someone on the street. Act swiftly. You have a seed that can get stolen. You will get talked out of it, people will think you are getting at them or you're a bit mad, but these are all lies and deceptions put there by the enemy. Just do it! The fruit will come. Be brave. You're a warrior for Jesus. The fruit (blessings) can only come with obedience.

6. AUTHORITY

Now all situations can be tackled with authority (God-given). Go into the world, accompanied by signs and wonders, healings, words for people on the street, and believe all things are possible in Christ. The key is to know who you are in Christ and only do that which you have been called to do.

CHAPTER EIGHT

Conquering Fear

How to recognise the different types of fear that may be holding you back from entering into God's purpose for you.

You are probably familiar with 1 John 4:16-18:

> *God is love. Whoever lives in love lives in God, and God in him. In this way, love is made complete among us so that we will have confidence on the day of judgement, because in this world we are like Him. There is no fear in love. But perfect love drives out fear, because fear has to do with punishment. The one who fears is not made perfect in love.*

However, many of us as Christians can become paralysed by fear. Fear is not of God; it is of the enemy and is specifically designed to render us immobile for as long as possible. We all feel it; even Jesus in the garden of Gethsemane went through a testing time of what He described as His soul being overwhelmed with sorrow to the point of death, just before He was crucified. But Jesus knew how it would end. He may have felt fearful, but He didn't succumb to His feelings. How did He know the ending? By reading biblical prophecy and communicating with His Father in prayer. Fear is irrational, because we know the end for us too, if we read the book. We are sons and daughters of the living God, and we are heirs who will rule and reign in a new kingdom for eternity. Read Daniel 7:27:

> *Then the sovereignty, power and greatness of the kingdom under the whole of heaven will be handed over to the saints, the people*

> *of the Most High. His kingdom will be an everlasting kingdom
> and all rulers will worship and obey Him.*

The difference is that Jesus did what He had come to do because He believed it. Nevertheless He still verbalised how he felt to his Father in Heaven. We too must be open and honest with God. He is our Father too and He knows how we feel anyway, but He wants us to trust Him.

Some of what we experience in this life is a test. I remember only recently feeling gripped by irrational fear. We were away on a weekend break in a caravan park in Cornwall. Where we were staying was quite a way out of town, right by the sea, and the caravan park was huge. During the night our youngest son began to get quite poorly with wheezing, coughing and difficulty breathing. Now, bear in mind that at home he often has had to be given an inhaler to assist his recovery when he gets a cold (although he's certainly not asthmatic). However, I suddenly realised that I had forgotten his inhaler in the rush to get away after work, and when he took a turn for the worse I began to panic. Through my mind went all sorts of scenarios which, if you're a mother, you will understand. My husband is Mr. Cool when it comes to dealing with a crisis, and he just said it would be fine. As my son continued to cough and splutter and we kept on cuddling and soothing him I suddenly came to my senses (or The Holy Spirit gave me a nudge) because I began to pray, and so did my husband. I prayed against the fear. I prayed in tongues and then prayed for him to get better – in that order, I think; it was all a bit of a blur! Anyway, he stopped coughing, I calmed, peace returned to me, and we all got a good night's sleep.

The point is, as Christian people we are in a relationship with God the Father. He made us. He made the world and He loves us so much that He wants us to trust Him with every part of our lives, especially the bits we find difficult. If we feel loved by Him, we will not be afraid to tell Him things and ask for help when we need it. So why don't we? Because at times fear can paralyse us or can block what God is trying to do through us on the earth (our assignment here).

There are many different types of fear, but they all fracture our union with God our Father. Many of them may keep us immobilised for all of our lives, but in prayer they can all be broken.

FEAR OF WHAT GOD WILL SAY IF WE GET CLOSE ENOUGH TO LISTEN

This type of fear occurs when we don't really want God to give us a way out of our present circumstances. We may listen to sermons about freedom and closeness to God, but we don't ever really open ourselves up to listening to Him because we like it where we are. We like it here, just the way it is on the earth, in this comfy place with plenty of stuff, a good profession and more than enough money to see both our children and ourselves all right until we get to Heaven. Remember the rich, young man in Matthew 19:21:

> *Jesus answered, "if you want to be perfect, go, sell your possessions and give to the poor, and you will have treasure in heaven. Then come follow me". When the young man heard, he went away sad, because he had great wealth.*

When we give our lives to Jesus, we have to be prepared to do some things that we may not think we want to do. But remember Jesus in the garden at Gethsemane. Nothing He will ever ask us to do will be beyond what we are capable of. It certainly will never be anywhere near as difficult as what Jesus did for us. His perfect love for us will cast out all fear if we let it. We have a choice, ultimately. It's a freewill gospel because God wants us to choose to trust Him to take care of our lives because we understand how much He loves us. When we give up our will and say, "Truly, your will be done on the earth," we will begin to live the life that God originally intended for us. Are you prepared for God to ask you to do anything for Him and the kingdom? What about if He asked you to sell up and share your possessions with the poor? Pray and ask God today what you're holding on to, and feel totally free in Him.

FEAR OF GETTING IT WRONG

Some people are prevented from entering into their inheritance in the kingdom and the promises of God because they don't want to get it wrong. Maybe God has been telling you for some time now to do something, but fear of failing stops you even taking a baby step towards it. The promise is there, but until you prove your faith by following despite the fear you are experiencing you will never know what was waiting, in other words what God had prepared for you in advance. Remember the children of Israel who never quite made it? God has great things waiting for us who believe, but we have to be prepared to get out of the boat. There have been several examples of God telling us as a family to do things which may at first have seemed odd, but God has always blessed us with positive growth either in our relationships, finances or ministry when we have obeyed.

As I'm writing this we are entering into another transition period in our family life. My husband is a builder and has been working quite happily for his uncle for some years now. A few months ago he had a strong sense whilst praying one day that God was telling him to step out on his own and become self-employed. He has waited on God, faithfully listening for a time to do this and was definite that God said April as the month to go for it! So, it's now the end of March and he has handed his notice in so that by April he will be out on his own. Bear in mind that he had no work lined up (except a couple of small maintenance jobs at church); he has no vehicle, no finance to back the business and has yet to set up insurances. Now, in a worldly sense it would seem like madness in this current economic climate to even think of doing this, but my husband has faith – bucket loads of it! Anyway, as a starter, the Sunday before he handed his notice in, a very dear friend of ours asked if Sam had any time to put up a fence and a shed in her garden, as she had come into some money. And I was able to say, "Actually he'll have all the time in the world in a month's time!" Also, one of our friends at the soup and tabletop evening we run at church said that he would like a large wood store built in his grounds and would my husband be available? That's now going to be his second job, and I expect his business to go on and prosper because there is nothing to fear if it's a plan of God's. He blesses us particularly when we listen and trust Him for all our plans in our lives. We believe God will provide, because He has told us to do it in the first place. The enemy may try to plant doubts and fears in our minds to stop it happening, but if we follow God's plan, however scary it may seem at the time, the fruit will always be there. Recognise God's voice over the enemy's by remembering that He has plans to prosper you. Say it out loud if necessary! God will provide.

FEAR OF WHAT OTHERS WILL SAY OR DO

This one can creep up on us regularly, if we're not careful! Imagine God wants you to speak to someone about Him (remember that's what we're here for, after all). It could be a work colleague or a neighbour or a family member, and let's just say that you decide not to do it. Does that mean that that person has lost their chance of salvation and that they will never hear the gospel just because you give in to fear? Just because you don't want to appear pushy or politically incorrect, look silly or be disliked, or whatever deception stops you? Honouring God is the most important thing in our lives as Christians, and by telling others we are honouring Him. Through that action we are showing Him that we care and feel loved enough by Him to want someone else (whom we love) to share it with us. We have to ask ourselves the difficult question, do we really love our family and friends? What if we pass up an opportunity of helping them into sharing eternity with us? We can't keep it to ourselves, because it means we are not flowing in God's love if we do. What's more, God will use another Christian who is functioning in the body of Christ to bring them in, and then you will be asked by your nearest and dearest, "You know Jesus? Then why didn't you tell me about Him?" We can be part of the flow of blessings and honour as long as we stay attached to the source, and remember that His perfect love casts out *all* fear. God just wants to bless you and me.

If you need any more persuading that this type of fear must not stand in your life then read what Jesus said to His disciples about it in Matthew 10:32:

> *Whoever acknowledges me before men, I will also acknowledge him before my father in heaven. But whoever disowns me before men, I will disown him before my father in heaven.*

Remember we are here to be a blessing, and because of the way the flow of the kingdom works (as God designed it) you also get blessed. Rather than always recounting how many times God has blessed us, perhaps we should start to really ask ourselves how many times we have blessed others this week. A simple prayer, which I have adopted every day, is to say, "Dear Father, who would you like me to bless today?" It works! (Thank you Joyce Meyer; I think that was one of yours!) Shift your mind so that you see yourself as here to be a blessing, and then you will be truly blessed.

I remember God gave me a picture once of a huge stadium filled with people, and as I was watching, coloured beams rained down onto their heads! I heard the words, "The more you bless, the more you will get blessed." I've always remembered that and try to find as many opportunities to help others as I can. It's amazing that getting your mind off yourself and more onto others helps you to dispel fear. My Mum always said, "There is always someone worse off than you." What a pearl of wisdom! I'll tell her one day!

FEAR OF GOD NOT SHOWING UP WHEN WE PRAY

This fear tends to come over us when we've prayed for things and our prayers are not answered in the way we thought they should be! It's amazing how many Christians fall into the trap of feeling fearful of praying because of this. We have to face the fact that God's ways are not always our ways, and we must not jump to that conclusion however tempting it may be because if you have no prayer life then your relationship with Father is fractured. This of course can happen when someone remains ill or even dies! God loves us, God answers prayer and God knows how long we have on this earth – we don't. We must keep an eternal perspective whilst we are living here so that we can enjoy every day as if it were the only one we have! God designed it this way, not us! He is the all-knowing creator; some stuff He chooses to let us in on now, some He will save until Heaven and some we will never know, because He knows best and He is God.

We must pray when someone gets sick because that's what He told us to do. How many mountains of sickness would never have been moved if we had not prayed? It's not that He couldn't do it without us but that His word says he wants us to go to Him in prayer. He gave us authority, and when we truly believe, great healings take place – we've witnessed them. But when it doesn't turn out our way we must learn to look for the blessings in the situation, however sad. I've seen dying people grow more spiritually than you would have ever thought possible; I've witnessed a person on life-support have experiences in the spirit realm; and I remember seeing a calmness I couldn't understand in someone who knew they were going to die. These are all examples of keeping a heavenly perspective whilst living on the earth. Eternity is in Heaven. There is no sickness in Heaven. There are no tears in Heaven. And when Jesus comes back, the Bible says in 1 Thessalonians that our relatives who have gone before us will meet us in the clouds with Him. We are only here a short time, to do God's will, so I for one am not wasting another second living in fear of unanswered prayer. I pray all the time and am confident that my God is answering my prayers, however He sees fit – 'cos He is God and I trust Him!

Remember Romans 8:28:

> And we know that in all things God works for the good of those who love Him, who have been called according to His good purpose.

There is always a blessing, but we don't always look for it hard enough. We don't always see it. God is love, so He always shows up – but maybe not as we expect. On the other hand, if He has given us authority over sickness and we exercise that authority but every time nothing happens, then it is time to go back to Him and ask, "Father is there anything in me that may be getting in the way?" If we are in God then the flow should be there, but we must not expect a formula to be present; it's more about trusting God's word above anything else and obediently doing it, regardless of the apparent outcome. He is not a God of confusion; He wants to grow our characters. We will only stay stuck if we choose to, but if we see this life as training for an eternity with Him we may be able to stay more positive and less fearful and never ever stop praying – that's our lifeline to our Father in Heaven.

FEAR OF GETTING HURT

We can place a hard case around our heart so that not even God can get in because of hurts from the past. We can become so afraid of being hurt again that we just harden our heart for protection. People may have wounded us (even in church), so we put up a protective shield so that no one can hurt us again. Sometimes we may open up a little bit of our hard heart to let someone in, but the minute they upset us or let us down we cut them off and say things like, "There, that proves it: I'm being too soft and people are just taking advantage of me." Soft-heartedness, or being vulnerable, is essential if God is to get in and heal broken-heartedness which is what many of us Christians suffer from. We put up a front and often use religious phrases which can convince people around us that we are all right, when in fact inside we are crying out to be healed and to be loved. Start with what you know. God loves you unconditionally. Whatever you've done, whatever you are doing and whatever you will do will never stop Him loving you. Study this love. Study the scriptures about His love. Play worship songs about His love. You have to get this. He sent His son to die for you; that's how much He loves you. If it were just for you alone, He would have done it so that you could be free – so that you could be free to love, free to laugh, free to dance and sing, skydive – whatever! – and enjoy this life in abundance. Because of Him, life is here now if you will only open yourself up to Him, open your heart to Him. The very first step is to let Him in, and then you will start to let others in.

Sometimes you may see Him in someone else. I did. My husband is a walking example of Jesus living in a human being, and he shows it by his kindness, his love, and his care of the family, his service to other people and in his patience and self-control. I know I'm biased now, but I wasn't when I met him. God changes us and moulds us to be more like Jesus so that others will see it and want it too. If we are paralysed by fear, others see that fear. We need to always stay close to God. Once you've softened and God has taken away the fear of someone hurting you, you will get to the point where, because you know you're loved by God, you won't care so much if someone hurts you anymore. Now you won't shield or harden your heart anymore; you will instead feel compassion for the other person. You may still feel hurt, but it won't damage you. You will accept it as part of life in the kingdom. After all, Jesus did warn us that people would hate us because of Him. The next lesson that God might want to teach you is about loving your enemies! What you must remember is that the world is full of others who want you to help them or want to hear about Jesus; even if some people reject you, you will be welcomed with open arms by others.

FEAR OF THE UNKNOWN

We're all right here, aren't we? We don't do any harm? We love the Lord, we love our church, we love our music, and we love our building. So what if people are talking about God doing a new thing? We've seen so many 'new things' come and go we're not sure if we want to try anymore or even if we have the energy! Sound familiar? This is dangerous talk, and this is why churches stay the same or even shrink (when folks die off).

This reminds me of a letter I received from a lovely lady once who had read an article I had written about Christian rock music for our church magazine. She was totally convinced that this music was of the enemy and that the Bible said there was only one way to worship God – in spirit and in truth – and so on… I remember feeling so sorry for her as she thought she was right because she took up her cross daily (her words) and denied herself (her words again). But the truth was she had totally missed the abundant life message of the gospel. God will always keep His children one step ahead of the enemy if we will only dare to keep Him close – so close that we can be receptive to His revealing new ways of treading the enemy underfoot (he's already beaten).

The enemy loves religion and 'pew potatoes' (James Rutz's words in 'Mega shift'); they are no worry to him at all. In fact he probably won't even mount an attack on them but leave them sitting there until Jesus comes back! The problem is that when someone is bound by religion, they actually believe that because they are not attacked it is evidence that they've 'got it'. We will never totally 'get it' until Heaven! We do need to grow up as Christians and see the truth, which is that if we are miserable, sick, disliking church and critical of our brothers and sisters then we are not doing God's work here on the earth and that is to shine, shine, shine! Standing in the fresh new wind of The Holy Spirit, which is blowing through the church at the moment, is just what is needed to blow away the cobwebs of religion and religious thinking and encourage people in church to join the party.

FEAR OF DYING OR LOSING LOVED ONES

This type of fear can grip people and is often the result of someone close to us dying whom we obviously love very much. We become unnaturally anxious and clingy. We try to hold on to those whom we love and can even inhibit their movements and freedom because of this fear. But we can never alter when someone is going to die, however unfair it may seem to us. The Bible tells us that our days are numbered. We are only here as long as God has predestined for us, and fear of dying will not stop it happening; it will just damage our life while we're here. Yes, there are instances when fighting a battle alongside someone who is sick seems like a defeat when they die, but we must always keep an eternal perspective. We probably see someone's physical healing as the most important thing, but does God see it that way, when He knows that our spirit will live with Him forever? Also, this type of fear can spread to other family members, particularly children who can learn this behaviour very early on in their lives and often think that this is quite normal.

The Bible says that angels can accompany those of us who believe, so God will even make sure (if we stay in Him) that we are supernaturally protected from dangerous situations. There are plenty of stories about angelic intervention and assistance even by armed angels (in both world wars, for instance). Once I heard about a woman who was walking home late at night. She passed a man who later got arrested for attacking a different woman. She was so interested to know why she wasn't attacked when the other woman was that she confronted the suspect with the question after identifying him in the police line up.

"Why didn't you attack me? I was alone just like the other woman."

"Alone?" he replied, "What about the two big guys who were walking with you?"

She *was* alone, so the other two must have been two protective angels sent by God. Awesome! What a faith-building moment for her, but also because she told her story we can also celebrate with her, for God's glory, and gain encouragement from it too.

Fear of the future, an unnecessarily long grieving period and being over-protective only lead to a sad, anxious life for both us and our family who still want to enjoy time together here. Life here is for living, and eternity is a long time to be with our loved ones who have already gone home. Jesus said, "So do not worry or be anxious about tomorrow, for tomorrow will have worries and anxieties of its own. Sufficient for each day is its own trouble." (Matthew 6:34, AMP).

This is a truth that really will set you free. Again, a song comes to mind, in conclusion[4]:

> *Even though I walk through the valley of the shadow of death*
> *Your perfect love is casting out fear*
> *Even though I'm caught in the middle of the storms of this life*
> *I won't turn back; I know you are near*
> *I will fear no evil*
> *For my God is with me*
> *And if my God is with me*
> *Whom then shall I fear? Whom then shall I fear?*
> *Oh no, you never let go,*
> *Through the calm and through the storm*
> *Oh no, you never let go*
> *Every high and every low*
> *Oh no, you never let go, you never let go of me*
> *You keep on loving me...*

Remember, if fear has existed for a long time in your life, it may help to ask a friend, pastor or elder at your church to pray with you and help you in bringing down this stronghold in your life. The most important thing is listening to God. Turn to Him, and He will always be there for you.

---

[4] 'You never let go' by Matt and Beth Redman (c) 2005 Thankyou Music

Out of the Pigpen!

CHAPTER NINE

It's Not How You Start

Finishing well. How to keep a heavenly perspective whilst living on the earth and how to negotiate the street maps on the earth and stay looking to Heaven.

Picture a main road with side streets and alleys along its length. Imagine that Heaven is at the end of the main road and that God's blessing and power is constantly flowing along this route. Living on this road is where we will find God's purpose for us here on the earth. We have been put in this place of light and favour, and it's here that we move from one level of glory to another until we get to Heaven. The Bible tells us that this road is narrow and few are those who walk it, and it's easy to see why this is such a powerful truth. It is so important in our relationship with God that we listen to where we are in this picture because the enemy will try to entice and keep us up a side street or alley for as long as possible – for life, if he has his way. When you stop and think what these deceptive side streets are it all becomes clear what God is trying to show us through this powerful image. These alleys or side streets are paths which lead us away from God and His purposes for us, such as religion, materialism, partying (which could lead to addictions), unforgiveness, abuse, the occult, permissiveness, career, family, self-importance, shopping etc.

The really great news of the gospel is that we can turn and repent at any time, come to the line at the junction of the main road and seek God's forgiveness and healing or deliverance and be back on the road which He had intended for us all along. This demands something of us; we may have to use our will to determinedly seek to do the right thing according to His word. We have to be obedient to the word in order to see a difference in our lives. We have to know that nothing is too difficult for Him and that there is nothing we can do that could separate us from the love of God. He is the same, always; we just have to learn to align ourselves with the flow of favour, blessings and power. Remember the story of the prodigal son, be honest with yourself, and know where you are. His precious Holy Spirit is with you always so that you will be progressively transformed into His likeness as He promises in His word.

Romans 12 talks about how we are all designed to be just one part of the whole body, each doing what He has given us to do for the benefit of each other. When you think about it, that would suggest us all moving along the same road! How can we, if we are still living on different streets – some of us in Party Avenue, others on Self-important Close, and many of us stuck in Materialism Road? It's time to get radical and move house so that the mighty army can be effective, fully equipped with all our different talents that God has given us for His glory and leave the stuff of this world behind. It's time to store up our treasures in Heaven, as that's where we will be for eternity, and not become too settled here. The most amazing thing is that as we've discovered many times when you do obey the call to follow Him and do His work, He blesses you with the things of this world anyway. *Seek first the kingdom...*

John 13 tells the story of Jesus washing His disciples' feet shortly before He died. Notice how many times the words 'knew 'or 'know' are used in this piece of scripture:

> *Jesus <u>knew</u> that that the time had come for Him to leave this world and go to the father. Having loved his own who were in the world, he now showed them the full extent of his love. (v1)*

> *Jesus <u>knew</u> that the Father had put all things under His power, and that He had come from God and was returning to God. (v3)*

> *For He <u>knew</u> who was going to betray Him (v11)*

> *Now that you <u>know</u> these things, you will be blessed if you do them. (v17)*

Apart from the obvious things that Jesus is teaching us here about the importance of being close to the Father as He was in order to do His will and the importance of being cleansed by the word of God constantly, I believe there is much more to this piece of scripture for us as members of His body today. Our churches are full of wounded warriors who shudder at the thought of one more battle! There are pews full of great men and women of God immobilised by past hits from the enemy, be it sickness, healings that didn't happen or relationships broken through church divisions. God wants to change that. He is calling us to fight a clean war with His weapons – together, in unity, serving each other as He did when He walked the earth over two thousand years ago, in order for us to begin to fulfil what it says in Ephesians 4:11-13:

> It was he who gave some to be prophets, some to be evangelists, and some to be pastors and teachers, to prepare God's people for works of service, so that the body of Christ may be built up until we all reach unity in faith and knowledge of the Son of God and all become mature, attaining to the whole measure of the fullness of Christ.

I believe there are things we can do in faith so that we can enter into this promise.

1. Know we're loved unconditionally
2. Let Him clean us
3. Stand shoulder to shoulder, all in the same place, doing our little bit
4. Know the enemy is beaten and that we can use His weapons of love to minister the various forms of grace which He gives to us. (Revelation received whilst reading God's word, prayer, healings, dreams, prophetic words, tongues, acts of kindness.)

James 4:8 further clarifies this.

> Come near to God and He will come near to you. Wash your hands and purify your hearts you double-minded...Humble yourselves before the Lord and He will lift you up.

We can only know our place and our bit in the body if we get closer in our own personal relationships with our Lord Jesus.

God's weapons today and how to use them

The well-known passage in Ephesians 6:13- says:

> *Therefore put on the full armour of God, so that when the day of evil comes you will be able to stand your ground, and after you have done everything, to stand. Stand firm then, with the belt of truth buckled round your waist, with the breastplate of righteousness in place, and with your feet fitted with the readiness that comes from the gospel of peace. In addition to this, take up the shield of faith, with which you can extinguish all the flaming arrows of the evil one. Take the helmet of salvation and the sword of the spirit, which is the word of God. And pray in the spirit on all occasions with all kinds of prayers and requests.*

Well, I believe all God is doing in these end times is reminding us of what we already have as Christians. He is simply giving us His weapons in a new language for this current age, but they have always been available to us, as the above scripture and many others throughout the Bible demonstrate. So, if we look at the 'new' weapons like *revelation through scripture*, is that not the same as using "the sword of the Spirit, which is the word of God"? Likewise, if we look at us *praying* for healing and seeing miraculous transformations take place amongst the body of Christ, is that not just taking up our shields of faith and standing on the truth of His word? We are now beginning to be radical believers of the word and praying scriptures like, "I speak to this mountain of sickness in the precious name of Jesus," or, "By His stripes, be healed." Also the interpretation of *dreams* is only what Daniel or Joseph did way back in biblical times, so why shouldn't God use them today to minister to both the saved and unsaved? After all, the entire gospel is a gospel of peace and love, and it is God's intention that none will perish and all His children receive the gift of eternal life with Him. Furthermore, all of these new initiatives such as street pastors, soup kitchens etc, that are seeing amazing fruitfulness, are they not just what Jesus did when He reached out to the lost with acts of kindness and love? The gospel of peace is to reconcile all men to God, and what better way is there for God's people than to copy Jesus' loving approach to our community? I think the more we show the outside world care and kindness, the more likely it is that they may venture back into our churches and find salvation.

Finally, a brief word about the huge breakthroughs that I believe are taking place when we actually use our God-given gifts, together to bring glory to God in these times. In Joel 2:28- the Bible says:

> *And afterwards, I will pour out my spirit on all people, Your sons and daughters will prophesy, your old men will dream dreams; your young men will see visions*

This book testifies to some great miracles that we have seen in our town recently, but I believe that we haven't even begun to see into the spiritual realm fully. However, during our joint church meetings in our town we have had many people sharing visions that they have seen; also we have had numerous prophetic words given to our church that have actually become reality in the natural as well as an increase in people's confidence in sharing and interpreting dreams in church. God is encouraging us to trust Him more and more for the answers to our dilemmas or decision-making in our everyday lives. We can trust Him for our finances, for our healing, for our families' salvation... But it is all about the relationship that develops between God and us whilst we are walking on this earth that He is concerned about. How we grow in Christ, becoming more like Him, is what it is all about; the more we see it the more we know it and the more we trust it to be true.

Furthermore, during some of our church's and joint churches' meetings the most contentious gift amongst Christians has been used to encourage many. I am, of course, talking about tongues, which although is spoken about many times in the New Testament, especially after Pentecost, is rarely discussed in many congregations. It's amazing how many churches are actually offended by the very mention of the word 'tongues'. (No prize for guessing who doesn't want this powerful weapon unleashed on him.) 1 Corinthians 14 has much to say about this, but in verse 13 it says:

> *For this reason anyone who speaks in a tongue should pray that he may interpret what he says.*

And that is exactly what God is doing in our meetings. For instance, only last week someone spoke in tongues and another person gave the interpretation, which was, "From Heaven I see you;

on the earth I walk with you." What a great encouragement to God's people and also what a great opportunity to give Him the glory here on earth when we talk to each other as brothers and sisters. Also, when interpretations are brought alongside the tongue, anyone visiting the gathering can also begin to see the power of God speaking to His people today.

Our small group of youth leaders have used the prophetic word to reach some of our young people who have attended our youth club recently. We have a small number of youngsters who have been attending our club for a couple of years. We have taken them on camps. We have brought them the gospel through activities, videos, YouTube clips, Bible quizzes etc., and we have got to know them really well. One day, during one of our regular prayer meetings where we ask God what to cover with the young people, He put it to us that we should ask for individual words for them. So being an obedient bunch we set up an evening where we played worship music, prayed and wrote down what God was saying to each of the seven young people. Wow! What He said was just awesome about how much He loved them, guidance for their futures, personality traits that only He could know and so on! Anyway, after a time of preparation in which we typed out their words in the form of a letter to each of them and following a discussion with them about what prophecy is, we gave the words to the young people. They are (all except two) non-Christians, but they were completely astounded how God could know such intimate details about them and were full of questions. We keep praying that God will continue to reveal more of Himself to them, through whatever means, so that more fruit is born for His glory in the church.

Another initiative which is bearing fruit in our town is called 'prayer in the square'. Again it is a joint initiative, with different churches joining forces to pray for people in the centre of town and to bless them. Many people have been healed, and we are expecting many to return to our church congregations as a result. More recently an even more exciting project has hit the streets where teams of treasure hunters ask God for descriptions of people out there who He would like to touch that day. (The people are the treasure.) It's incredible how specific these can be. For example, one Saturday morning a team received a word from God that there was a man outside a particular shop in town in a wheelchair and that he needed prayer for a bad back. Just as He said, there was the man, and the team dutifully engaged with him and prayed for him. Obviously, at times, the fruit of these encounters may be immediately evident or we may never actually know what happens, but we must trust that God knows and loves every single one of these people and it is that very special revelation that may lead them, sometimes unbeknown to us, to give their lives to Jesus at some time in their life. I can assure you that it's a very exciting step to take, if not a little scary.

The point is that God has assignments for every one of us here on earth, and He can only work through us if we will be prepared to listen, obey and act ridiculously for Him once in a while. In fact one of my favourite Christian songs has the lyrics,[5]

> *I will dance, I will sing to be mad for my king*
> *Nothing Lord is hindering the passion in my soul*
> *And I'll become even more undignified than this*
> *Leave my pride by the side.*

Christian life is certainly not dull and boring as some like to think. If we will only set our minds and hearts on doing His will, we will have enough excitement to last a lifetime.

---

[5] Extract taken from 'Undignified' by Matt Redman (c) 1995 Thankyou Music

Out of the Pigpen!

Chapter Ten

God is Good and He is Jealous for Me

Obedience is everything. "What did Jesus do?" How to use Jesus as a model for our lives when the going gets tough.

God's will and purposes for us are good and will not change. They stay the same, whether we choose to obey or not. Deliverance and healing are still on His heart for His children, even if we do not acknowledge it happening. Obedience is everything. He is jealous for me!

When the two Marys went to Jesus' tomb in Matthew 28, they and some soldiers had a divine encounter that produced two very different reactions. When the angel had appeared to them and given instructions as to what the two Marys should do, the scripture says, "They left the tomb hastily with fear and great joy and ran to tell the disciples."[6] Notice they are instantly obedient and then they meet Jesus on the way and throw themselves at His feet. He calms them; He is with them as they go. This is so relevant for us today. How can we learn from this obedient reaction? When God tells us to do something, how much easier it is when we do it straight away, without dawdling or being slow enough to allow the enemy to steal that seed which has just been planted in our hearts. Now look at what happened to the soldiers who also witnessed that same awesome event outside the tomb.

---

[6] Matthew 28:8 (AMP)

Verse 11 says:

> *While they were on their way, behold some of the guards went into the city and reported to the chief priests everything that had occurred. And when they had gathered with the elders and had consulted together, they gave sufficient money to the soldiers.*

So the soldiers bowed to the trappings of the world and allowed themselves to be persuaded that what they witnessed was not as important as becoming wealthy. This again is so relevant today, because it is actually what happens to many of us in our Christian lives. We allow ourselves to be taken away from Jesus by listening to our friends or sadly, at times, leaders in churches who then persuade us that our interests would be better served by doing what they tell us to do. At times we can even begin to doubt that which we heard from God in the first place.

However, when we do believe what we hear from Him and act swiftly upon it, we get the reward of amazing fruitfulness in our lives, just as in this story when Mary told the disciples faithfully. They reached Jesus at the mountain in Galilee (verse 16) where He had directed them. Furthermore, they received an amazing word on that mountain which still stands for all of us who call ourselves His followers today.

> *Go then and make disciples of all the nations, baptising them in the name of the Father, and of the Son and of the Holy Spirit. Teaching them to observe everything that I have commanded you, and behold, I am with you all the days to the close and consummation of the age.*

What a promise! Why would we want to do anything but obey? It's because the deceptions of this world become so convincing that we end up getting deceived into doing the things of this world and become further away from God, and His voice therefore becomes fainter and fainter. I have found that to stay close to God requires using your will to make yourself read, worship, pray and meditate on God each day to stay receptive to His voice. When temptation or words of condemnation come in (which they will) you are then able to simply say, "Away in the name of Jesus!" and stay strong and unaffected by the ways of this world whilst still living in it. We are called to be in the world but not of it.

Jesus was the only perfect example of this, so if we study what He did when He walked the earth then we can learn to live more successful lives as Christians. If we look at the gospels there are so many examples of Jesus doing the right thing, according to His Father's will, even when He didn't feel like it or was under Satan's attack. Because He was the perfect human being (God in fleshly form) He always got it right. We are not, so we cannot get it right every time, but we can study and learn and call upon the power of the Holy Spirit in us to help us be more successful at doing God's will and fulfilling our purpose, even when it feels wrong. We cannot trust our feelings, but we can trust God's living word of truth. In Matthew's gospel alone, we can learn so much how to act, by reading and doing what Jesus did.

Matthew 4:1 tells us of when Jesus was led by the Holy Spirit into the desert to be tempted for forty days by the devil. At this time He quoted God's word every time the enemy tempted Him.

> *Jesus answered, "It is written: 'man does not live by bread alone, but on every word that comes from the mouth of God' (v4)*

> *Jesus answered him, "It is also written: 'Do not put the Lord your God to the test.'" (v7)*

> *Jesus said to him, "Away from me, Satan! For it is written: 'Worship the Lord your God, and serve Him only.'" (v10)*

He sees the enemy off with scripture, and we can do the same by our very nature. If we truly believe that Jesus came to live in us when we were born again and if we really believe that His name is above any other, then we can tell the enemy to go, use Jesus' name and quote scripture to stop the attack. So why don't we? Why do we often wait until we are under the weight of struggles or sin or sickness before we even think of doing what Jesus did? Because we don't always recognise the deception of the enemy. That's why he's called 'the deceiver' – we often don't know we are being deceived until the fruit of the situation shows us. This is where the body of Christ is so important to us. Our brothers and sisters are indispensable at helping us to recognise a deceptive situation or stronghold and they can pray for us as well as discipline us through speaking the truth in love. Many times someone lovingly telling me God's word and showing me what the Bible says about a particular situation has brought me to my senses. Trusting in God's word and also trusting in each other as fellow members of Christ's body is what ultimately can be the difference between succeeding or struggling in our Christian walk.

So what happened to Jesus after He had quoted scripture to the devil in the desert? See verse 11 again in Matthew 1:

Then the devil left Him, and angels came and attended him.

Wow! We can all learn short scriptures to speak out when times are tough (although we all have our own personal strengtheners). Why do you think the enemy doesn't want us to learn scripture and will try any underhand method possible such as tiredness, lack of time, boredom etc. to paralyse this powerful tool in the Christian's arsenal of weapons? Because he understands the power that is in it. We can pray about this, asking the Holy Spirit to take away any distractions and to guide us before the reading begins. For example we could pray something simple like, "Please help me, Holy Spirit, to receive revelation through reading your precious word today. In the name of Jesus I cut off any distractions such as tiredness or apathy. Thank you, Father. Amen."

I believe Jesus is waiting for us to take responsibility for our walk with Him and to really believe that what He did for us on the cross made us able to take authority over the enemy. After a time of doing this, the attacks seem to be easier to recognise and deal with. The enemy is already beaten – Jesus did it – we simply have to believe it and do what Jesus is telling us or showing us through His word. We can't be surprised if we are leading fruitless, Christian lives if we haven't done the basic things that the Bible tells us to do. It's fun to learn, and the more you read the more you receive through revelation in the scriptures. Sometimes I actually find myself saying, "Oh yeah! Thank you, Lord! I didn't see that before, but now I do." Then you won't be able to stop yourself telling someone else, and so the encouragement and strengthening of His body builds and grows and the enemy's hold gets weaker and weaker.

When Jesus began His teaching, healing and ministering, Matthew tells us how everywhere He went He talked about the kingdom. He taught about who would be blessed, and He further clarified the Ten Commandments (chapter 5). He not only teaches us here that we are salt and light in the world but how we are in need of a saviour. We can talk to our friends and family this way by discussing the Ten Commandments and appealing to their conscience, which is as close as the unsaved get to the Holy Spirit. He taught us how to pray and how to act (chapters 6 and 7). We are told of His compassionate healings and deliverances (chapters 8 and 9). He gave authority to His disciples, which I believe is for us too when we are born again (chapter 10), and we too can pray for our sick friends or relatives. What better way could there be for God to be given the glory here on earth than to demonstrate His love by supernatural healings? After all, it's pretty difficult to deny the power of our Lord when this takes place and our relatives can come to know Him too and enter into the kingdom by experiencing His miraculous healing power. It's all about love! We cannot keep this to ourselves; we have to do the work we were designed to do and honour God, by bringing Him glory and spreading the good news. Look at Matthew 10:32. These are Jesus' words:

> Whoever acknowledges me before men, I will also acknowledge him before my Father in Heaven. But whoever disowns me before men, I will disown before my Father in Heaven.

After this, Matthew discusses the parables which Jesus taught the disciples and describes yet more miracles such as the loaves and the fishes. Then He begins to warn about people and situations to be aware of (chapters 23 and 24), such as the Pharisees and the signs of the end of the age. But it is in chapter 26 that we see an amazing demonstration of how to act when faced with obeying God's purpose for our lives or following the ways of the world. This is our greatest challenge, I believe, as Christians today. He had to admonish His disciples for not staying awake to help Him pray at this critical time in Gethsemane. Jesus fell with His face to the ground and prayed.

> My Father, if it is possible, may this cup to be taken from me. Yet not as I will, but as you will. (v39)

> Then He returned to His disciples and found them sleeping." Could you men not keep watch with me for one hour?" He asked Peter. "Watch and pray so that you will not fall into temptation. The spirit is willing but the flesh is weak." (v40)

> My Father, if it is not possible for this cup to be taken away unless I drink it, may your will be done. (v42)

Out of the Pigpen!

The keys here are to look at what Jesus said about the spirit and the flesh. If we feed our spirit through prayer in relationship with God (who other than Jesus knows what God said to Him in those intimate times in prayer in the garden?)[7] then we can be confident and strong enough to do God's will even if it is difficult! We can be sure that when we listen to what God is saying to us in meditative prayer, during worship or when reading the Bible, we will move forward into our intended inheritance just as Jesus did. After all, what God asks us to do according to His will for us will never be equal to what Jesus chose to submit to on that cross to secure our freedom and eternal future.

---

[7] If you read Luke's account of Jesus in the garden (Luke 22:43), you will recall an angel visited Him to give Him strength.

CHAPTER ELEVEN

Our Covenant Relationship

The Jesus culture. How to spot the deceptions which may keep us bound.

James 4:4 talks of how breaking that covenant with God is like an unfaithful wife, having affairs.

> *...do you not know that being the world's friend is being God's enemy? So whoever chooses to be a friend of the world takes his stand as an enemy of God.*

It is so easy to be deceived in this area of Christian life and to see other cultures as being particularly corrupt. Take Africa, for example, and the corruption that is rife in that society. I have experienced western preachers urging Africans to live according to the Bible and advising them that lying and cheating is abhorrent to God. This is true and is often due to spiritual attacks increased by the presence of occult activity. However, what we often fail to understand in the west is that we break that covenant with God too but in a more covert way! Materialism, self-righteousness, political correctness, permissiveness, religiousness, and using alcohol as a crutch, etc. (anything that is contrary to the word) take us away from the Father's care by our choice. The only difference is that the enemy is being culture-specific in the way he operates, and we are deceived into believing these are all acceptable. The Bible is the same worldwide, so maybe we should see Christianity as the 'Jesus culture'. This may prevent us from seeing other cultures in the third world as inferior to ours here in the West. In actual fact, the simpler our lifestyle, the less likely we are to be distracted from our purpose in the kingdom. I've discovered that usually whatever we teach others God tests us on. So if we are teaching purity and covenant relationship with God, we have to check ourselves in the light of the Holy Spirit to make sure we are aligned with the Father in our own lives.

The Jesus culture

The Jesus culture is what we need to build. We are in a battle, but we must learn the rules of engagement and follow the commands of the commander.

- Get clean – get the stones out of the jars; unblock the wells. (This means allow the Holy Spirit to gently convict us and help us to remove old habits, sins or dysfunction from past relationships that may be within us, so that we can be filled completely afresh.)
- Stand firm, using your weapons given by God. (Know the enemy is defeated.)
- Understand God's way of fighting is to love Him, love yourself and love others. (Remember the two commands that Jesus gave were to love God and your neighbour as yourself.)
- Move forward, doing good (whatever His purpose is for you).
- Remember signs and wonders accompany those who 'go' (a by-product of a life lived according to His purpose). They are just the start and they are for the unsaved more than for us. Yes, they confirm our faith (what we already know), but they reel in the unsaved.
- Do not think the warm glow is 'it' (the presence of God experienced by us all at some times during our Christian lives). That's when we get delivered or healed, transformed by the power of His spirit.

CHAPTER TWELVE

The End Time Church

How to be a disciple today and obey the call of Heaven, whilst bearing fruit on the earth.

We are the end time church

Revelation 3:14 reads:

> *And to the angel (messenger) of the assembly (church) in Laodicea write: These are the words of the Amen, the trusty and faithful and true Witness, The Origin and Beginning and Author of God's creation: "I know your [record of] works and what you are doing; you are neither cold nor hot. Would that you were cold or hot! So because you are lukewarm and neither cold nor hot, I will spew you out of my mouth..."*

This is widely preached by biblical experts and prophetic people as representing the church today – the church of the end times. At first it seems a harsh piece of scripture, but in actual fact it is enormously reassuring to us and gives us the clear instructions we need to fight the enemy in the end-time church.

This is a time of preparation for God's people. We need to get into our purpose in the kingdom now, in churches all over the world. He is the commander of the army, the head of the church. He knows me and my gifting and you and yours. He has put us together on purpose, and if we do what we have been called to do, we will be blessed with His promises. Only do what you have been called to do. Ask Him what your bit is! Get into His purpose for your life. Take your place in the army and you will be safe in His care. He can only do what is right – and righteousness will be blessed. He cannot act unrighteously, so if He has asked you to do something and you refuse then He cannot bless that unrighteous, disobedient action

Complaining that we are stressed, overworked, and sad or struggling financially is not being filled with peace, joy and love. In essence, this is what God wants for you. This is the disciple lifestyle.

There is only one way to check if you are aligning yourself with this move of God, and that is to check your fruit. Matthew 7:15-23:

> Beware of false prophets, who come to you dressed as sheep, but inside they are devouring wolves. You will recognise them by their fruits. Do people pick grapes from thorns, or figs from thistles? Even so every healthy (sound) tree bears good fruit [worthy of admiration], but the sickly (decaying, worthless) tree bears bad, (worthless) fruit. A good (healthy) tree cannot bear bad (worthless) fruit, nor can a bad (diseased) tree bear excellent fruit [worthy of admiration]. Every tree that does not bear good fruit is cut down and cast into the fire. Therefore you will fully know them by their fruits. (AMP)

If you come to church each Sunday, get a warm glow, then go off back into worldly temper tantrums, stress, desiring material stuff, drinking... then you're trying to fit God around your life. Crisis living – only calling on God when we are struggling – is not the Christian life. He knows how to build a church. Do your bit faithfully, with love, serving others. His plan was edification, so that we can serve others. Ephesians 4:11-13:

> And Christ gave gifts to people-he made some to be apostles, some to be prophets, some to go and tell the good news and some to have the work of caring for and teaching God's people. Christ gave those gifts to prepare God's holy people for the work of serving, to make the body of Christ stronger. This work will continue until we are all joined together in the same faith and in the same knowledge of the Son of God. We must become like a mature person, growing until we become like Christ and his perfection. (NCV)

Obedience always bears fruit. Try it. Test God in this. Take a word that He's given to you and do it. He will give you power and authority if it's of Him. He will bless it and the fruit will be there. If you don't do it or if something is not of Him there will be no fruit. You have lost nothing but could gain a lot for yourself and others around you.

All the bubbling over of blessings and miracles, which result from obedience, are for the outside world. When they see it they will not be able to say no. Jesus' first words in ministry reported in Matthew 4:17 were "Repent for the kingdom of Heaven is near." In Matthew 10:1 Jesus called his twelve disciples to Him and...

> *He gave them authority to drive out evil spirits and to heal every disease and sickness.*

And he said in verse 7:

> *...as you go preach this message, the Kingdom of Heaven is near.*

Pray today. Ask God what your purpose is. What if your purpose is blocked? Ask Him; He will tell you.

There is a way back to the Father. He is looking for you.

Out of the Pigpen!

PART II

Exploring Deeper

Further topics for Bible study and spiritual growth

Out of the Pigpen!

CHAPTER THIRTEEN

The Star of Bethlehem

The star: a sign of the times. How to know your place.

A sign of the times

Matthew chapter 1 tells the Christmas story. All of the events are the fulfilment of prophecy. Isaiah 7:14:

> *Therefore the Lord himself will give you a sign: The virgin will be with child and will give birth to a son, and will call him Immanuel.*

So the story unfolded, and now we are part of the world's story. The star, which lit the sky and led the wise men to the stable, was a sign of light in the sky, and God put it there on purpose for them to follow. Since we are New Testament followers of Jesus, we are the light of the world (Matthew 5:14).

All of the people in the story were obedient to the words of God received in dreams, visions or angelic appearances, and they were blessed in their lives. Would Jesus not have come if the wise men hadn't obeyed and followed the star? It will all unfold as it is written, whether we do our part or not. There is not one type of human condition, problem or situation that isn't covered in the Bible. We are in there, near the end, and the end has been written. To fulfil our destiny in Christ we must follow Jesus just like the kings and the shepherds followed the star. Look to Him.

The plan doesn't change. Herod opposed it, but it was prophesied he would. You may decide to turn away from God, but Jesus knows as He said that the love of many would grow cold, and we have the teaching about 'the prodigal son'.

We weren't there to follow the star like the kings; we didn't listen to Jesus preach on a hillside or get miraculously healed by Him. We didn't witness the crucifixion or talk to Him on the road following His resurrection or get filled with the Spirit at Pentecost, but we are a covenant people, spirit–filled, a new creation and part of the end-time church. We are the city on the hill, the light of the world, and we have been called to preach the gospel. What an exciting purpose we have, and now is the time to rise up and do it.

What is your purpose? What gifts has God given you to use for His glory to be re-established on the earth before He returns for His bride, the church? The end has been written; it's up to you whether you accept the blessings on offer. We can be for Him or against Him, as He prophesied when He walked the earth. Jesus even prayed for us before He left us, as written in John 17:20-26:

> *My prayer is not for them alone. I pray also for those who will believe in me through their message, that all of them may be one, Father, just as you are in me and I am with you. May they also be in us so that the world may believe that you have sent me. I have given them the glory that you gave me, that they may be one as we are one.*

Furthermore He also told us that signs and wonders would accompany those who do the Father's will, so what a great time to be on the earth! This has all been made possible because Jesus chose to go to the cross in obedience, therefore sending the Holy Spirit to live in us, to be our comforter and to cause us to grow through gentle conviction and love.

Chapter Fourteen

The Legacy of Jesus' Words

Jesus' parables. What did He say the kingdom of Heaven would be like?

Have you ever really focussed on Jesus' words and realised how awesome it is that He was speaking about us and to us, way back when He was walking the earth over two thousand years ago? Look at Matthew 24:3- and marvel again at how accurate His words were about the signs of the end of the age, and just watch and see how things are unfolding around us, just as He said they would. I not only believe in Him, I believe Him and what He says above any other person.

In the parables He says that we who are in the kingdom will understand what He says (Matthew 12:10). We learn how we will be when the kingdom comes. We are all on a journey, and we are all at different stages of that journey. God is doing something new with His people at the moment. One of these things is learning to be obedient to the word as well as an increase in the use of the prophetic word spoken to those in the church and out on the streets. Also signs and wonders such as miracles, healings, visions and angelic appearances, loving and caring for people out in the community and revelations through prayer are more frequently spoken about (Matthew 13:52).

> He said to them, 'Therefore every teacher of the law who has been instructed about the kingdom of heaven is like the owner of a house who brings out of his storeroom new treasures as well as old.'

These are being given as tools for defeating the enemy and also so that more and more people will come to salvation.

Jesus tells us in the parables what the kingdom of Heaven is like... These stories all stand for attitudes that will be developed in His people before the end of the age.

Look at Matthew 13:24-:

> *The kingdom of Heaven is like a man who sowed good seed in his field. But while everyone was sleeping his enemy came and sowed weeds among the wheat and went away.*

The weeds are explained in verse 39 of the same chapter as being sown by the enemy but living amongst us. Here we are being urged to repent and accept Jesus as the only way to being on the kingdom side rather than working in opposition to God.

Now look up these other parables:

The mustard seed and yeast spoken of in verses 31-33 refer to how our words can make the kingdom grow when we speak about God to our friends and family.

The treasure and the pearl in verses 44-46 refer to how we should invest in God and live for the kingdom.

The fishing net parable starting at verse 47 talks about what happens when we are not doing as we should be doing as Christians and urges us to be obedient to God.

The landowner parable in Matthew 20:1-16 is a warning about people who grumble about those who have been saved after them receiving the same reward. We are encouraged here to be happy for everyone who is saved

The unmerciful servant in Matthew 18:21-35 explores how people can still be harsh and unforgiving towards each other even though the basis of the Christian faith is being pardoned by God for our past despite not deserving it. So, we are taught here to be forgiving of others as we have been forgiven.

The owner of the vineyard in Matthew 21:33-43 is all about those who are entrusted with God's work but fail to produce any fruit, and it is clearly speaking to us and advising us to do according to our purpose for us.

The king who prepared a wedding banquet in Matthew 22:1-14 especially ministers to those who are too busy with their own lives in the world to do what God wants them to do – so it's teaching us to be selfless rather than selfish.

The ten virgins in Matthew 25:1-13 tells of those who are ready and those who are unprepared when the bridegroom arrives. It speaks to us about the need to prepare ourselves now, as we don't know when he'll come.

Finally, *the sheep and the goats* in Matthew 25:31-46 is about the people who have and haven't helped those who are less fortunate than themselves and also how each of us is accountable to God for what we did with our salvation. We are urged to treat everyone as if they were Jesus Himself. (Matthew 25:40 says, "I tell you the truth, whatever you did for the least of these brothers of mine, you did for me.")

We will bear fruit in our attitudes as we allow the Holy Spirit to gently change us. He will convict us and mould us if we use our free will wisely and allow this change to happen by opening our hearts and minds.

If we conform to this process, the people in God's kingdom will be selfless, obedient preachers of the gospel. We will be *sowing, living* God's way, *forgiving* and *celebrating* the salvation of all people whom God calls. We will be *fruit-producing, listening* and *obeying,* prepared *multipliers* who are *caring* and *generous* to God. I believe that when we in the church are truly transformed we will see a dramatic rise in the number of people coming to Christ (a combination of all the parables' fruit as Jesus taught us).

Out of the Pigpen!

Chapter Fifteen

The Legacy of Jesus' Resurrection

How to understand that we are now the plan and recognise the Holy Spirit is with us. A lesson in surrender from Jesus in the garden of Gethsemane.

All aspects of Jesus' life and death were prophesied events; all according to God's plan. Even the Pharisees respected the prophetic word. We live in a different time where this is seen as odd; also we are over-analytical. We have dwelt in the church for too long on the piece of scripture which warns of false prophets, and the fear of getting it wrong immobilises us. We have been given discernment, so if we know a word is from God (we've discerned it) we need to believe it will happen, as in Jesus' day.

The plan is the plan. We can't change it; it has already been planned! In fact, *we are* the plan. God had a purpose for Jesus and He has a purpose for all of us. Jesus told the disciples in Acts 1:8 to start their ministry with Jerusalem, then Judea, then Samaria, then to go to the ends of the earth. We will all be working in different places but with the same plan (to bring in the lost). Our own family and close friends will be our Jerusalem, Judea is like our workplaces, Samaria could represent our towns, and the ends of the earth I believe might be our overseas missions in the body of Christ.

Mark 16:9- is an important scripture, which teaches us how the disciples turned their unbelief into action:

> *After the Lord Jesus had spoken to them, he was taken up into heaven and he sat at the right hand of God. Then the disciples*

went out and preached everywhere, and the Lord worked with them and confirmed his word by the signs that accompanied it. (v19-20)

Notice they were unbelieving *but* they soon got over it. This is an encouragement for us – even people who saw, talked to, ate with and indeed lived with Jesus and heard from His lips firsthand what was going to happen to Him struggled, so we shouldn't be too hard on ourselves. God is merciful; we condemn ourselves. Get over unbelief and 'get on and do'! We can't do it when we have gone to Heaven!

The power of the Holy Spirit came down when Jesus went up. The disciples went out and the lost came in. We all have a mission. Listen, He will give us power and courage. Believe in and live His words for us – prophetic and in the Bible – and we will have a great life and bear fruit for His glory, here on the earth.

Surrender for Easter

When we read about the disciples in the garden of Gethsemane we have to wonder at just how much of what they had seen and done with Jesus had really sunk in. Just like the children of Israel who had witnessed amazing signs and wonders and had received such divine assistance from God Himself both coming out of Egypt and whilst in the wilderness. They just didn't get it (except for Joshua and Caleb). The Israelites came out into the desert and then they died through fear, unbelief, murmuring and lack of faith before reaching the Promised Land

The events in the garden of Gethsemane occurred on the night after Jesus had demonstrated foot-washing; it was a test to see if the disciples had 'got it'. Jesus was asking them in essence to wash *His* feet, and at first it's a bit shocking to see their reaction when He asked them to keep watch whilst He went off to pray in His hour of need. What did they do in response to His request? They fell asleep! Had He not just demonstrated serving each other by washing their feet? He knew their weaknesses. That's why He told them to pray. Praying is a direct line to the Father and is something spiritual, hence the reason Jesus said, "Pray so that you will not fall into temptation."(Matthew 26:42)

He also told them that the spirit is willing but the body is weak, and this is a key for us as New Covenant Christians. You have to see that the disciples at this stage were not New Covenant people – they were trying to keep awake under their own strength. We have the Holy Spirit to help us avoid giving in to temptation. He is our comfort, our support, and our lifeline. Once we have been born again, then we can choose to feed our spirit through spiritual things like prayer, worship, reading and studying God's word and have power to defeat the attempts of Satan who will try anything to disconnect us from the Father's love.

However, if we are worldly Christians who may attend church but don't live Jesus' way the rest of the time, we may as well be Old Covenant people because we have become detached from our power source and are living by the enemy's rules, not God's way. This type of life becomes frustrating and fruitless. We become discouraged and start to complain just like the children of Israel. It is an act of will to obey God, just as Jesus did in the garden when He said, "Not as I will but as you will."(v.39) This is what we need to say more often and pray in the Spirit so that we will be given the strength to not do as we feel but according to our purpose in Christ, as written about in the word. It is then that the power and blessings are evident. Look at Luke's account of their time in the garden and you will see how God answered Jesus' prayer – by sending an angel from heaven to comfort Him (Luke 22:43). Even after that He still sweat blood, he was feeling so anxious, but feelings did not stop Him doing what was right. Even if you're disappointed that no one seems to be there to wash your feet and you feel alone, as long as you are linked to the Father through prayer then help is always with you whatever the circumstance – but you must remember to pray. Feelings don't stop you doing what is right, that which God has told you to do. Now that you have the Holy Spirit you are never alone.

One further bit of encouragement when you look at Jesus' disciples' lives is to remember that they did become New Covenant Christians at Pentecost... big time! They got filled with the Holy Spirit, spoke in tongues, had tongues of fire on them and so on. Nothing held them back once they had the Spirit. What's stopping you? It's never too late. We can grow very quickly in the kingdom if we only learn to get closer and closer to God and become tuned in to His voice above all the others that demand our attention. Once we can hear, then we simply need to obey that voice. Just watch how quickly you will go from one level of glory to the next! The more you feed the Spirit, the weaker the demands of the flesh become, until eventually you will no longer notice the things that used to keep you bound. So pray with me...

> *Lord Jesus, I know that you died for me and love me with an everlasting love. Thank you for forgiving me my many sins from the past. Please help me to put my will aside and surrender to you, as I know you have a great future for me. Your kingdom come, your will be done in my life from this day forward, and change my mindset if necessary. I surrender it all to you to use for your glory. Amen.*

CHAPTER SIXTEEN

Ephesians 1 and Beyond

How to see the sermon as a seed and read, read, read!

Ephesians 1:3-8

Praise be to the God and Father of our Lord Jesus Christ, who has blessed us in the heavenly realms with every spiritual blessing in Christ. For he chose us in him before the creation of the world to be holy and blameless in his sight. In love he predestined us for adoption to sonship through Jesus Christ, in accordance with his pleasure and will—to the praise of his glorious grace, which he has freely given us in the One he loves. In him we have redemption through his blood, the forgiveness of sins, in accordance with the riches of God's grace that he lavished on us...

I was listening to a sermon one day, delivered by a very knowledgeable elder, teaching on Ephesians 1. He told us that in verse 4 we are "chosen", and in verse 5 we are "adopted as sons through Jesus". He said that we are "loved" as we are told in verse 6, that "in Him we have redemption through his blood" and that "He has made known mysteries to us". After church, I became aware of a sense in my spirit that this was just a starter. In fact I really felt driven to look in my Bible at the rest of the chapter. How did I know to do that? It's so hard to describe God's voice. It's not like it was a booming shout in my ears or anything; it was simply like my own thoughts. It was like I was thinking to myself. I've come to recognise this as the still small voice of the Holy Spirit, growing me on into a bigger pot! (Excuse the analogy if you're not a gardener, but when a seedling outgrows its pot, you transplant it into a bigger one.) Yes, the message I heard in church was sound, biblical teaching, but it was just the start, just a seed which God's spirit would feed and nourish into something bigger – a seed which could maybe then be passed onto someone else and become an encouragement to them or even grow into a piece of knowledge that could lead to someone getting saved.

I obediently looked up the rest of the chapter and discovered verses 13 and 14 telling about us being marked with a seal, the promised Holy Spirit, and verses 18-21 discussing us knowing of his incomparably great power for us who believe and that power being like the working of his mighty strength. Wow! We all have these gifts given by his grace. We all have the Holy Spirit so that we don't have to get stuck going around our own personal mountain one more time!

We are all in this personal relationship with Jesus and His Father, who is also *our* Father, so when we are prompted to study something further, or change an attitude, turn from destructive relationships or habits, we can trust it is because it will change us for the better and it will help us to move from one level of glory to another. It also means that we will shine brighter for Him in the world – and, after all, that is what we are here for.

This has taught me now that if I feel a little distracted during a sermon or frustrated that a lesson feels not quite right then I am to ask why. Just by having a positive mindset, rather than a negative one, shuts the door on the enemy and allows a situation that could have caused me to murmur or complain in the past to be transformed into a tool for my good. After all, doesn't Romans 8 say that all things work together for the good of those who love him and have been called according to his purpose?

CHAPTER SEVENTEEN

Preach the Gospel

How to understand why we are here and recognise and fulfil our assignment on the earth.

How often have you spoken to someone who you feel is spiritual? It seems like they are speaking the very words of God. Well, they probably are because they probably manage to stay attached to Heaven whilst functioning on the earth.

Jesus said, "As you go, preach this message: the kingdom of heaven is near."[8] Well, since He went it's here. We just need to believe it for ourselves and tap into the awesome power which is already waiting and has been won for us.

The enemy wants us (particularly young people) to stay away from the Bible. So he will sabotage any attempts to read it. Tiredness, boredom and irrelevance to today's society are all tricks used in our thought life to prevent us knowing the perfect will of God, as written in His word. But we must encourage each other to get into the secrets of God (revealed only to His people) by living the gospel lifestyle as an exciting choice, because the more we read, the more we know God as our Father and appreciate how much He loves us and wants to cheer us on from one degree of glory to another.

Check yourself. How far have you come in the last year? How much have you allowed the Holy Spirit to convict and change you from one level of glory to the next? We often stay stuck because we don't recognise God's voice and confuse it with the condemnation of

---

[8] Matthew 10:7 (NIV)

the enemy. Close the door on his attacks in Jesus' name and only listen to the loving words of God, which will help you to grow and get better. If it builds you up (even if it's disciplining you) then it's God. If it knocks you down then it's the enemy.

When you receive a revelation of who Jesus is, it then becomes impossible not to tell people because it is embedded within you. You believe it, and so it is real to you, and when something becomes real to you then you just have to tell people.

CHAPTER EIGHTEEN

Believe His Words about You

How to select scriptures about you to meditate on... and enjoy strengthening who you are in Christ. How to see yourself as God sees you.

The Bible is full of encouraging words about who we are as God's children. I remember selecting these awesome scriptures and sharing them one Sunday morning in church. When we read them, meditate on them and even stick them on post-it notes around the house, something shifts in our minds, and revelation of who we are begins to dawn on us. I know that when I am having a difficult time either through illness or during a trial of some kind, these words remain the same. The truth is always there, and who I am in Christ never changes, regardless of the circumstance. Let these life-sustaining words sink into your heart. They are for all of us as Christians, and believing them is a huge key to living the life Jesus died for us to have – an abundant one.

JESUS DIED FOR US

Romans 8:34
Christ Jesus who died – more than that, was raised to life – is at the right hand of God and is interceding for us.

Out of the Pigpen!

GOD GAVE HIS SON FOR US.

John 3:16
For God so loved the world that He gave His one and only son, that whoever believes in Him shall not perish but have eternal life.

WE HAVE BEEN CHOSEN, REDEEMED AND ARE CHILDREN OF GOD

1 Thessalonians 1:4
For we know, brothers and sisters loved by God that He has chosen you.

Luke 1:68
Praise be to the Lord, the God of Israel, because He has come to His people and redeemed them.

John 1:12
Yet to all who did receive him, to those who believed in His name, He gave the right to become children of God.

WE ARE NEW CREATIONS

Galatians 6:15
Neither circumcision nor uncircumcision means anything, what counts is the new creation.

HE HAS REMOVED OUR SINS FAR AWAY FROM US.

Psalm 103:12
As far as the East is from the West, so far has He removed our transgressions from us.

WE HAVE POWER OVER THE ENEMY

James 4:7
Submit yourselves then to God, resist the devil and He will flee from you.

WHEN WE PUT ON GOD'S ARMOUR WE CAN RESIST THE ENEMY.

Ephesians 6:13
Therefore put on the full armour of God, so that when the day of evil comes, you may be able to stand your ground.

OUR FAITH CAN MOVE MOUNTAINS

Mark 11:23
I tell you the truth if anyone says to this mountain, "go throw yourself into the sea" and does not doubt in his heart but believes what he says will happen, it will be done for him.

CHRIST LIVES IN US

Romans 8:10
But if Christ is in you, your body is dead because of sin, yet your spirit is alive because of righteousness.

WE ARE PART OF HIS BODY HERE ON EARTH

Romans 12:5
So in Christ we who are many form one body and each member belongs to all the others.

MIRACULOUS SIGNS ACCOMPANY US WHO BELIEVE

Mark 16:17
And these signs will accompany those who believe. In my name they will drive out demons, they will speak in new tongues...they will place their hands on sick people and they will get well.

THE SPIRIT LIVING IN US IS GREATER THAN THE ONE IN THE WORLD

1 John 4:4
You dear children are from God and have overcome them, because the one who is in you is greater than the one who is in the world.

WE HAVE BEEN GIVEN GIFTS

1 Peter 4:10
Each one should use whatever gift he has received to serve others, faithfully administering God's grace in its various forms.

WE HAVE BEEN HEALED BY HIS WOUNDS

1 Peter 2:24
He Himself bore our sins in his body on the tree, so that we might die to sins and live for righteousness; by his wounds you have been healed.

Out of the Pigpen!

These words were specifically chosen to encourage and build up the church at a time when we were learning about our identity in Christ and they contributed to many of us gaining real revelation for the first time of who we are. Equally, if we are struggling or simply need clarity in other areas of our lives, we can always use His word (The Bible) to minister truth to us. Money issues, temptations, parenting, loving the unlovable can all be tackled by trusting in His word and selecting appropriate scriptures to meditate on. Try it for yourself, and your mind will be renewed just as we are promised.

CHAPTER NINETEEN

Apart From Him we can Do Nothing

How to stay attached to Him and remember prophetic phrases to keep our Heavenly (eternal) focus.

How many times as Christians do we receive prophetic words either individually or as a church and simply file them and put them on a shelf? These words are promises from God, and they are meant to be read often, prayed about regularly and believed, even when circumstances may seem otherwise.

We received this word once as a church:

> *There are words on the shelf, gathering dust. Get them down, look at them again. Step out in faith and the fruit will come.*

This encouraged us and others in our church to look at words that had been spoken over our children, and we took out the words from our son Jude's dedication service from after his birth. We looked at them afresh and prayed them again for him, and we now do this regularly. These are words spoken over Him that will shape his future, and they shouldn't be hidden; they are there to build our faith and encourage us as a family.

> *God is the same yesterday, today and tomorrow, like a horizontal line across a page. Where are you? Check yourself regularly against the line. Why? It's good to see yourself in the light of God's word and His Holy Spirit during prayer times.*

This word came at a time when we needed to demonstrate to our youth group the importance of staying close to God, and we got them to all plot where they thought they were in their life in relation to the 'line' in this word (we had a large piece of paper with a straight line across the middle). It was a good time of activity and discussion with our young people. We often repeat the same activity with the group, and it helps them to self-check and recommit to Jesus if necessary.

Here are some more prophetic words that are relevant to all of us as Christians. It may be good to spend some time praying into their significance in our lives, as we move forward believing He will transform our lives, the local church, our communities and the world.

> See yourself as God sees you – a king, a priest and a son/daughter of the living God.

> We need to shift our minds so that we see ourselves, each other and the unsaved as God does.

> Miracles are a by-product of a life lived according to His purpose, obedient to his word.

> When we are all using our gifts amazing things will happen.

> Your salvation will lead to good works, which will lead to unity.

> Words from God are precious jewels. We need to wear them like a necklace always.

> The most important people in the church are those who have not come in... yet!

> A time will come when selflessness will replace selfishness in the church. We need to say, "Note to self: go away!"

> Jesus went up, the Holy Spirit came down, the disciples went out and the lost came in.

Chapter Twenty

More to Come

The 'more' is a taste of what we've seen already. How to believe that God is at work here on the earth... now! Recall those miracles!

Whilst out street pastoring at one o'clock in the morning, we were amazed when talking to a uniformed police officer to discover that there were six of us regularly walking the streets! Bear in mind that officers are trained to observe things more closely than the rest of us. After telling him that we always work in teams of four, he continued to argue that he had seen six! Angels accompany us on duty, how fantastic is that! And they must wear uniforms, too.

After praying the Lord's Prayer with a seriously ill friend (God indicated that this was needed) and after sharing in a time of confession and repentance, we saw an inch taken off her cancerous tumour.

Following the laying on of hands and prayers for my Dad, lying in critical care, I witnessed his face change from grey to pink, just like the mercury moving up a thermometer! Incidentally, he described a place with forests, beaches and lakes with a peaceful feeling after he came round. He went back into this state a week later and went to be with His God, but now I know where he is and that he's at peace.

We have experienced numerous occasions of instant healings of serious back conditions, severe sickness bugs and seasonal coughs and colds.

On one occasion, our whole family was being sick in the middle of the night, but when my husband said, "We are all children of God.

You don't belong in this house. Enough! Go in the name of Jesus!" we were all instantly and completely free of the sickness.

After three nights of persistent coughing, I was given a picture of a mountain with rocks being thrown at it. When the tickle came in my throat during the night I just pictured the mountain (I guess the mountain was the cough), and said, "Go away!" in my mind as I imagined the rocks hitting the mountain. Needless to say my husband woke in the morning and commented that I hadn't coughed all night, and furthermore that was also the end of the cough!

During a meeting a few years ago, Daryl Stott was preaching, when silver dust began to appear on the palms of my hands. As I dusted it off, more appeared for a couple of hours. A week later my teenage son gave his life to Jesus.

We have collected many photographs of angels (orbs of light) surrounding us during meetings in our little church. They seem to be most evident in times of joyful worship or wedding celebrations.

During Soul Survivor youth music festival in the summer of 2010, we witnessed three boys in our group receiving spiritual healing. They had visions of Heaven; there was sobbing, laughing and subsequent peace and healing from grief following bereavement of both parents and abuse in the family. The young people then testified and encouraged members of our church when they returned home and have demonstrated a real and lasting growth in their faith since then, with two of them serving in the worship team on guitar each week and the other bringing words of knowledge.

Whilst praying for one boy at our youth club who had back pain (we had sat him on a chair and noticed that he had one leg shorter than the other) my husband, two other leaders and I felt and heard a pop as his shorter leg grew. After commenting, "That felt weird!" in typical teenage style he jumped up and said his back felt better. Later that evening he phoned to sign up for a Christian camp that we were taking kids to this summer (as he's not yet a Christian)! God is so good! All the time!

Once we led a youth meeting at our house, and after talking to the young people about the power of the Holy Spirit vs. alcohol (some of them had experimented with their friends at a party), the presence of God came down so strongly during the singing that many of us began dancing and singing. Many of the youngsters even went out and danced in the street! What more evidence did they need that God's spirit was present and was free and only did them good!

A recent miracle (at the time of writing) was when I was suffering with pain in my elbow (tennis elbow, I think) and my husband asked our youngest son Jude to "pray for Mummy". He laid his hand on the painful arm and prayed that Jesus would make Mummy's arm better. It was instantly pain free. If only we could all live with simple faith like that – the faith of a little three-year-old child! I'm sure when we do we will see more miracles happen.

Even more recently our youngest son got taken into hospital with breathing difficulties, and as the word was passed down our prayer phone line and people began to pray, his oxygen levels went from the eighties to a hundred percent in a matter of hours. What an awesome God!

Finally, at Soul Survivor and following another 'silver on the hands' manifestation during the prayer before we left, another 'babe' joined the family! One of the non-Christians who came along with us gave her life to Jesus and is now attending our church. God is good... all the time.

Out of the Pigpen!

CHAPTER TWENTY-ONE

Remember the Heroes of the Faith

Heroes past and present. Inspirational words from great men and women of God. How to gain encouragement from others' stories of faith.

When we read about other peoples' journeys of faith and even hear about the struggles they may have had along the way, it can inspire and motivate us. This may happen at a time when we could need encouragement or a breakthrough. Here are some of the inspirational poems, stories and extracts that have done just that for me! Some of them I've shared when ministering to young people and others I've read out in church to build up the body. I hope you enjoy them too and find them inspiring as we carry on this exciting journey together for Him.

Two poems by Simon Guillebaud[9]

A Zimbabwean martyr wrote the following before he was killed:

I'm part of the fellowship of the unashamed.
I have the Holy Spirit's power.
The die has been cast. I've stepped over the line.
The decision has been made - I'm a disciple of His.
I won't let up, slow down, back away, or be still...
I will not flinch in the face of sacrifice,

---

[9] Poems taken from 'For what it's worth' © Simon Guillebaud 2006, Monarch books (a publishing imprint of Lion Hudson plc). Used by kind permission.

hesitate in the presence of the enemy,
pander at the pool of popularity,
or meander in the maze of mediocrity...
I am a disciple of Jesus.
I must go till He comes,
give till I drop,
preach till all know,
and work till He stops me.
And when He comes for His own,
He will have no problem recognising me...
my banner will be clear!

We don't want to be saying this poem at the end of our lives:

To sinful patterns of behaviour that never get confronted and
changed,
Abilities and gifts that never get cultivated and deployed-
Until weeks become months
And months turn into years,
And one day you're looking back on a life of,
Deep, intimate gut-wrenchingly honest conversations you never
had;
Great, bold prayers you never prayed,
Exhilarating risks you never took,
Sacrificial gifts you never offered,
Lives you never touched,
And you're sitting in a recliner with a shrivelled soul,
And forgotten dreams,
And you realise there was a world of desperate need,
And a great God calling you to be part of something bigger than
yourself-
You see the person you could have become but did not;
You never followed your calling.
You never got out of the boat.
(Author unknown)

The three-legged dog

I heard this story on a Cross Rhythms radio programme and I often use it to show young people how awesome God's prophetic insights are, today.

A chap was sitting reading his Bible on an aeroplane when another passenger asked him what he was reading. He said it was just a cookbook. The other man stated the obvious by replying, "No it's not – it's a Bible," and said something rather dismissive about it. The man with the Bible prayed, "Please give me something for this man that will show you are real to him." He was very surprised when God said, "Ask him if he likes animals," which he did. When the guy said, "Yes," the evangelist was slightly encouraged and was urged by God to step out further and specifically ask if he liked small dogs like Jack Russells. The sceptic began to get reeled in and asked, "How could you have known that?" And this is what God told the Christian to say:

"Well, many years ago you had a Jack Russell who was in a car accident and had to have his leg amputated, and while you were sitting in the vet's waiting room you prayed to God and said, 'If you save my dog's life I will give my life to serve you.' Well, your dog recovered and lived a full life with three legs; your prayer was answered and God wants you to know He is still waiting!"

Needless to say the man gave his life to Jesus there and then. Maybe God wants you to give words to people you meet out on the street. It can often be all that's needed to convince someone that God loves them!

Praying in delay, and tipping the bowls of heaven[10]

> I could go on and on explaining instances when I believe that God was waiting for prayers to be stored up in heaven in order to release enough power to do the job. Why did it take Jesus three hours in the garden of Gethsemane to break through? Why didn't angels come immediately and comfort Him? Because power was being released in the spirit to cause breakthrough.

> Why did it take a month to get rid of the cyst on my wife's ovary? Because power that was being released in the realm of the spirit was accomplishing something physically inside of her. Every day when that power was released, it was destroying the cyst just a little bit more and more...and more.

---

[10] Extract from 'Getting in God's Face' by Dutch Sheets p.143
Copyright 2006 Gospel light/Regal books
Ventura CA 93003
Used by permission.

Why did I have to pray for more than a year for the comatose girl I told you about at the beginning of the book? I went to see her once a week for a year, speaking the word of God, weeping, calling forth a new brain inside of her head and fighting the good fight of faith. Why did it take a year? Because it takes a lot of power to form a new brain. Why didn't God do it instantly? I don't know. I tried everything to get Him to do so.

I did all the things I read about the great heroes of faith doing. In faith, I even sat her up in the bed and commanded her to wake up; but like a limp rag doll, she flopped back down on her pillow. I don't know why God chose not to do it as an instant miracle; but because He didn't, I'm relatively certain of this: A measurable amount of power had to flow until there was enough of it to produce that miracle.

Clearly the power source – God - isn't the problem here. Ephesians 3; 20-21 gives us a clue as to what's holding up the process;

Now to Him who is able to do exceeding abundantly beyond all that we ask or think, according to the power that works within us, to Him be the glory in the church and in Christ Jesus to all generations forever and forever. Amen.

Notice that verse 20 says that God is going to do way more than we could ever imagine "according to the power that works within us". That means that however much power we have stored up in us, that's the amount that can be released or distributed through our prayers. If we're low on power, then we can't expect our prayers to move mountains. It's foolish to think we'll see miracles when all we do is mutter a routine two minute prayer every once in awhile before school starts or flippantly toss up a few words to God throughout the day. We have to release the power of God inside of us on a consistent basis.

As we do this, the scriptures indicate that our prayers accumulate. There are bowls in heaven in which our prayers are stored. Not one bowl for all of them but "bowls". We don't know how many, but I think it's very likely that each of us has our own bowl in heaven. I don't know if it's literal or symbolic. It doesn't matter. The principle is still the same. God has something in which He stores our prayers for use at the proper time:

And when He had taken the book, the four living creatures and the twenty four elders fell down before the lamb, having each one a harp and golden bowls full of incense, which are the prayers of the saints (Rev. 5;8)

And another angel came and stood at the altar, holding a golden censer: and much incense was given to him, that he might add it to the prayers of the saints upon the golden altar, which was before the throne. And the smoke of the incense, with the prayers of the saints, went up before God and out of the angel's hand. And the angel took the censer: and he filled it with the fire of the altar and threw it to the earth; there followed peals of thunder and sounds and flashes of lightening and an earthquake (Rev. 8; 3-5).

According to these verses, either when He knows it's the right time to do something or when enough prayer has accumulated to get the job done, God releases power. He takes the bowl and mixes it with fire from the altar.

I want you to picture this; He takes the same fire that fell on Sinai, the same fire that burned the sacrifice consuming the rocks and water and everything else when Elijah was on the mountain, the same fire that fell at Pentecost, the same fire that destroys His enemies, the very fire of Almighty God and He mixes your bowl of prayers with His fire! Then He pours it upon the earth- lightening starts to flash, thunder crashes, the earth quakes. Something awesome happens in the realm of the spirit that then affects the natural realm...

I hope this doesn't alarm you. I get excited when I think about it. I didn't know it at the time, but when I was standing over that comatose girl, every time I spoke the name of Jesus, every time I prayed in the spirit, every time I laid hold of God's word and promises, every tear I shed was put in a bottle (see Ps. 56:8)- or a bowl- and God was just watching until it was finally full.

And on a Saturday morning, the Almighty looked over at one of the angels and said, "see that little girl over there whose brain is no longer functioning and that has to be fed through her stomach and breathe through a hole in her throat and is lying there like a living dead person and the doctors say there's no hope and is going to die? Do you see her? Take this bowl that's been filled, mix it with my fire and go dump it on her head.

Out of the Pigpen!

An extract from 'Mega shift'

This amazing book of God's miraculous works on the earth today is by James Rutz.

Grind-it-out Obedience

The first catalyst of miracles is simple obedience.

A distinguished Indian evangelist named Sadhu Chellappa was on a mission trip to a village north of Madras, when in the middle of the night he suddenly sensed God speaking to him: Leave this house quickly and run away!

Not exactly a convenient thing to do. But Chellappa was used to accepting even strange instructions from the Lord without discussion, so he quickly dressed and ran into the darkness.

After a while he was in open country. Then as he passed beneath a large tree, he felt God tell him, "stay here and start to preach!"

Now even for an experienced evangelist this was puzzling- there was no one to be seen. Why did God want him to preach to an empty field in the middle of the night? But he stopped under the tree and began to preach the gospel.

Finally he reached the point at which he called on his unseen listeners to give their lives to Jesus. He was surprised to hear a voice from the top of the tree and see a man climb down crying.

He tearfully gave his life to Jesus. When Chellappa asked why he was in a tree out in the middle of no-where, the man admitted, "I came out here to hang myself"

Obedience is everything.

Epilogue

We are not alone in this battle. We have been put alongside other men and women in the body of Christ, whatever country we are from here on earth. We serve the same God, we believe the same things, and we love one another. So depend on your Christian friends when you feel weak or sick and need backup in prayer. We only have one enemy, and we all know what his mission is; the most important thing is not to get isolated or proud or competitive or deceived into thinking we are fine just as we are. I believe we all need to remember we are on a journey to a very special, amazing place. We have a great, eternal future, but we can have a fantastic fun-filled, action-packed life every day as long as we stay attached to the commander of the army. And I, for one, am having the time of my life! When I look back over my life, as well as enjoying seeing the victories that God brings here with us as his co-workers (and heirs) through signs, wonders, salvations, healings and deliverances, I will look up and say, "Lord I have no regrets; I gave you my all." When we stand before Him, we all would love to hear those amazing words, "Well done good and faithful servant." Let's give Him the glory here on earth for the great life we have through Jesus Christ, and believe me, there is no better life. So here's to the next year! Bring it on, as we take the Lord's battle to the streets of our towns, cities and nations, and bring His glory down onto the earth! Amen.

Appendix

My Personal Testimony[11]

I was christened as a baby into the Methodist church and always attended Sunday school and youth church each week with my family up to the age of eighteen. My parents lost confidence in the church we were attending, and I began to question several hypocritical actions of many of the members – and we decided to leave. It was at this time I left for university, and although I always considered myself a Christian, I did not attend church. It's important to say at this point that my understanding was that because I was christened as a baby that made me a Christian!

I was married for fourteen years to an extremely violent man, both physically and emotionally, but I stuck firmly to my vows, as I believed them to be binding. I also had two children by this time. I believed they needed both a mum and dad.

My mum died after a year long struggle with cancer, but I had a vision as she left this world which confirmed that the Lord was still with us as a family. Life became increasingly difficult without her, and I always knew that something was missing from my life as I struggled with life's blows. I finally gained the strength to 'go it alone' for the sake of my children and following a series of harrowing incidents in my own home. Peace began to return to my life after my abuser was removed from the house, but the stress at times was overwhelming, coping alone with my two children, and the rest of my family living three hundred miles away. I felt so alone at times, but I was determined to persevere and worked hard to return to teaching; I even dug gardens to pay the mortgage. I was Mum and Dad to the children for nearly five years and working so hard meant that I didn't have the time to think about what had happened to me.

Gradually, I began to build up a new social life and took up my old sporting pursuits. I made many new friends but much of this life involved partying, drinking and clubbing at weekends, when my

---

[11] This was written just after I got saved

118

children were away visiting their dad. I told myself that I needed this release valve and thought that I deserved it after working so hard, but many of the people I met only wanted to avoid problems in their own lives or to take advantage of others' weaknesses, so I quickly realised that it was a lifestyle that was of little interest to me. I met someone very special, however, on these outings to the pub that made me think very differently about life, and as we became friends he began to share his beliefs with me and explained how important his Christian faith was to him. Having met so many shallow, self-absorbed people, it was so refreshing to talk to someone who had a strength and inner calm that was unmistakeable.

As we got to know each other, we realised that we had so much in common and that we would always be friends. He took me along to his home group, where I was quietly welcomed and where I felt totally at ease. The people from his church were so friendly and open about talking through life's issues, and I quickly realised that the Bible means just as much in today's society as it did all those years ago. I began to read it when I felt stressed, dealing with the fallout and repercussions for two children, coping with having parents leading very different lives apart and the two sets of rules that needed to be mastered and understood. As I read I began to feel the most amazing peace and warmth from inside, and I knew that God was beginning to soften me from within. I also knew that he was really there and that he would lead me when I was ready. I entrusted him with my prayers. As my relationship developed with my future husband, we talked about this happening for me when the time was right, but it was a few weeks later and following more prayer times with God that I had the most amazing experience.

We were attending our local, monthly youth music event, and whilst singing I suddenly received a clear signal from the Lord that filled me with the most incredible warmth ever. There was no audible voice, no shining vision, no heavenly music, but I just knew at that moment it was time to give my life to Him – He was calling me. I looked at my boyfriend straight after I had said in my head that I accepted Jesus into my life, and although no words were exchanged, he knew too as the singing continued. After the singing had finished I told him that I was ready and that I didn't want to wait any longer. As we sat in the prayer corner with some church youth leaders, arms around each other, reciting the believer's prayer, I felt light, as if my troubles had been lifted and I was emptied and filled with God's love.

During chats with my home group leader, he put it to me that I would need to find forgiveness for my ex-husband, who had caused me so much harm in the past. I knew this would be my most difficult test, but by reading the Bible a lot and more silent prayers, I finally decided to hand him over to God. My life is full of positive experiences: good times, great friends, a fantastic new husband (we married in 2006). Why would I want to continue to try to make sense of my past? That part of my life is now in God's hands. I've come to understand that we are all judged by Him for what we do, and as I and my loved ones are in the Lord's care then I have nothing to fear anymore.

I have peace in my life, and God knows I have been given the strength to forgive. He knows it is He who has given me that strength and that I will always do His work from now on, whatever that may be, and looking back is not an option or indeed my intention. The way is forward as I learn more every day and go about life's challenges with joy and enthusiasm. (Since writing this I'm now a mother again to three-year-old Jude, praise God).

I know God loves me, unconditionally, and I want to live according to His will for the rest of my days. Since then, I still have stuff to deal with, but when I do it's with renewed strength, calmness and knowledge that I not only have the best, most supportive husband anyone could hope for but also the power and love of the Holy Spirit within me. I thank God each day for guiding me to my husband through life's circumstances and he in turn for leading me back to the Lord. We are now even stronger as a couple because we share so much more and we can face life's challenges on the same straight path together (we are street pastors in our town and serve in youth ministry together at church), sharing in the excitement and unparalleled joy that being a Christian brings.

Oh, and I have to say that I share who I am and what has happened to me with pride and tell everyone who will listen what my faith means to me! (This testimony appeared in our church magazine, which gets delivered to thousands of homes in our town). My Christian and non-Christian friends listen and celebrate with me that my life has changed – and who knows, I may be able to bring some of them along with me into the kingdom.

My favourite scripture at the moment is:

Matthew 5:10 (AMP)
Blessed and happy and enviably fortunate and spiritually prosperous (in the state in which the born-again child of God enjoys and finds satisfaction in God's favour and salvation, regardless of his outward conditions) are those who are persecuted for righteousness' sake (for being and doing right), for theirs is the kingdom of heaven!

Bibliography

God is our Father

1 Samuel 3:10-end
Matthew 10:32-end

The Starting Line

Matthew 24:4-13

How to get Born Again

John 3:3-7
1 Peter 1:3
1 Peter 1:23
Luke 7:36-50

God in a Box

Ephesians 3:20
2 Corinthians 10:4-5

People-Pleasing

Jonah 1:1
Matthew 12:48
John 14:16

The Journey of the Christian

Revelation 12:10

Conquering fear

1 John 4:16-18
Daniel 7:27
Matthew 19:21-22 (NIV)
Matthew 10:32-33 (NIV)
Romans 8:28 (NIV)

Matthew 6:34 (AMP)
Song: Matt & Beth Redman, "You never let go",
    (c) 2005 Thankyou Music

It's Not how you Start

Romans 12
John 13:1-17
Ephesians 4:11-13
James 4:8-10
Ephesians 6:13-18
Joel 2:28
1 Corinthians 14:13
Song: Matt Redman, "Undignified", (c) 1995 Thankyou Music

God is Good and He is Jealous for Me

Matthew 28
Matthew 4:1-11
Matthew 10:32
Matthew 26:39-42
Luke 22:43

Our Covenant Relationship

James 4:4 (AMP)

The End Time Church

Revelation 3:14 (AMP)
Matthew 7:15-23 (AMP)
Ephesians 4:11-13 (NCV)
Matthew 4:17
Matthew 10:1
Matthew 10:7

The Star of Bethlehem

Isaiah 7:14
Matthew 5:14
John 17:20-26

Out of the Pigpen!

The Legacy of Jesus' Words

Matthew 24:3
Matthew 12:10
Matthew 13:24-end
Matthew 18:21-35
Matthew 21:33-43
Matthew 22:1-14
Matthew 25:1-13
Matthew 25:31-46
Matthew 25:40

The Legacy of Jesus' Resurrection

Mark 16:9-end
Mark 16:19-end
Matthew 26:42
Luke 22:43

Ephesians 1 and Beyond

Ephesians 1

Preach the Gospel

Matthew 7:7

Heroes of the Faith

"For what it's worth; a call to no holes barred discipleship",
    Simon Guillebaud, Monarch books, UK 2006.
Story of the three-legged dog, Cross Rhythms radio, Plymouth UK
"Getting in God's Face", Dutch Sheets, Regal Books, 2006.
"Mega shift", James Rutz, Empowerment Press, 2005.
My testimony
Matthew 5:10 (AMP)

Contact the Author

To contact the author, please write to:

Jo Wright
7, Springhill,
Tavistock, Devon
PL19 8LB

Or send an email to:

jotheauthor@yahoo.com

Related Books from the Publisher

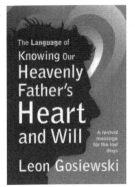

The Language of Knowing our Heavenly Father's Heart and Will

Leon Gosiewski

- Why are so many people leaving the church?
- Why are we largely bereft of God's power?
- If God is speaking, why are we not hearing?
- Is the Church in harmony with what the Bible teaches about it?
- Do we need revival?

Addressing these and other pertinent questions head on, the author unpacks what the scriptures have to say about knowing our heavenly Father, Jesus and the Holy Spirit on a relational level. Common misconceptions and unhelpful teachings are highlighted, and there is a call to return to a walk of holiness in which God is truly honoured as Lord and Saviour.

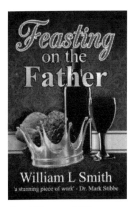

Feasting on the Father
William L. Smith

The Bible is essentially a love story – a book that reveals the heart of a Father towards his children. God does not keep his distance from us, nor is it his desire to punish us. On the contrary, his love compelled him to send his only son into an imbalanced world – to suffer in our place, and to bring us back to the Father as royal sons. Now, we are welcome to the table of the King of Kings...

This book is centred on Song of Solomon chapter 2 and reveals the heart of a loving Father throughout the scriptures. The truths explained in this book have the power to change your life. Once you have feasted on the Father, you will not want to look back...